C000149803

# Dorset
# NATIONAL TRUST
# Guide

# RODNEY LEGG

**Dorset Publishing Company**
WINCANTON PRESS, NATIONAL SCHOOL, NORTH STREET,
WINCANTON, SOMERSET BA9 9AT

For **Hazel Burns**

First published 1992. Copyright Rodney Legg
© 1992. All rights reserved.
Typeset by Bookman Limited, Merrywood
Road, Bristol BS3 1DX with layouts by Sandra
Goodman.
Printed by the Alden Press at Osney Mead,
Oxford OX2 0EF.
Distributed in Dorset by Maurice Hann from 36
Langdon Road, Parkstone, Poole BH14 9EH
(0202 738248).
International standard book number [ISBN]
0 948699 35 3

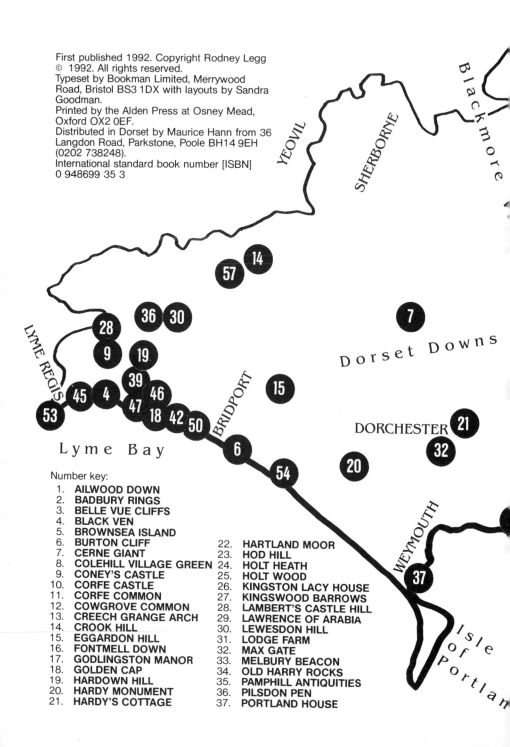

Number key:
1. **AILWOOD DOWN**
2. **BADBURY RINGS**
3. **BELLE VUE CLIFFS**
4. **BLACK VEN**
5. **BROWNSEA ISLAND**
6. **BURTON CLIFF**
7. **CERNE GIANT**
8. **COLEHILL VILLAGE GREEN**
9. **CONEY'S CASTLE**
10. **CORFE CASTLE**
11. **CORFE COMMON**
12. **COWGROVE COMMON**
13. **CREECH GRANGE ARCH**
14. **CROOK HILL**
15. **EGGARDON HILL**
16. **FONTMELL DOWN**
17. **GODLINGSTON MANOR**
18. **GOLDEN CAP**
19. **HARDOWN HILL**
20. **HARDY MONUMENT**
21. **HARDY'S COTTAGE**
22. **HARTLAND MOOR**
23. **HOD HILL**
24. **HOLT HEATH**
25. **HOLT WOOD**
26. **KINGSTON LACY HOUSE**
27. **KINGSWOOD BARROWS**
28. **LAMBERT'S CASTLE HILL**
29. **LAWRENCE OF ARABIA**
30. **LEWESDON HILL**
31. **LODGE FARM**
32. **MAX GATE**
33. **MELBURY BEACON**
34. **OLD HARRY ROCKS**
35. **PAMPHILL ANTIQUITIES**
36. **PILSDON PEN**
37. **PORTLAND HOUSE**

# Map of National Trust Dorset

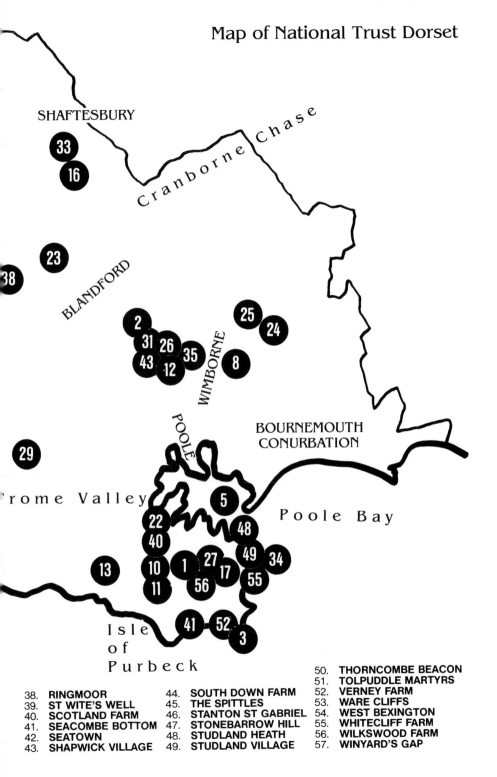

SHAFTESBURY

Cranborne Chase

BLANDFORD

WIMBORNE

POOLE

BOURNEMOUTH
CONURBATION

rome Valley

Poole Bay

Isle
of
Purbeck

38. **RINGMOOR**
39. **ST WITE'S WELL**
40. **SCOTLAND FARM**
41. **SEACOMBE BOTTOM**
42. **SEATOWN**
43. **SHAPWICK VILLAGE**

44. **SOUTH DOWN FARM**
45. **THE SPITTLES**
46. **STANTON ST GABRIEL**
47. **STONEBARROW HILL**
48. **STUDLAND HEATH**
49. **STUDLAND VILLAGE**

50. **THORNCOMBE BEACON**
51. **TOLPUDDLE MARTYRS**
52. **VERNEY FARM**
53. **WARE CLIFFS**
54. **WEST BEXINGTON**
55. **WHITECLIFF FARM**
56. **WILKSWOOD FARM**
57. **WINYARD'S GAP**

*Introduction to this book and* **National Trust Dorset**:
The Trust was founded on 16 July 1894 at the Duke of Westminster's sumptuous town-house, Grosvenor House in London's Park Lane, by **Miss Octavia Hill, Robert Hunter** (not yet knighted) and **Rev Hardwicke Rawnsley** (not yet Canon). It was incorporated as **The National Trust for Places of Historic Interest or Natural Beauty**, initially "as an Association not for profit under the Companies Acts 1862 to 1890", and given parliamentary protection in 1907.

As for what has become a massive presence on the ground in Dorset, it sprang from a handful of little acorns, to base the metaphor on the Trust's oak-sprig logo and its omega signs.

Three of the Trust's smallest properties were its first in the county, starting with the **Hardy Monument** (to Nelson's captain rather than the author). This was held on lease from 1901 and purchased in 1938. Second, though appropriately the first freehold land to be acquired in Dorset, was the chalk-cut **Cerne Giant** hill-figure; given in 1924. Thirdly, to commemorate the centenary of the **Tolpuddle Martyrs**, their village green came into ownership in 1934.

Those three properties, together comprising little more than an acre, were the sum total of the Trust's Dorset holdings prior to the gift of the late **Lawrence of Arabia's Cottage** just before the outbreak of the Second World War.

The entries in this book, under the sub-heading of Trust ownership, outline the rapid growth in the estate, which by 1992 had escalated into an area in excess of **21,000 acres** – which is about **thirty-three square miles** and makes the National Trust by far the biggest single landowner in the county.

**Entries here are alphabetical: clustered where geographically appropriate, and at other times sub-divided into manageable entries, with cross referencing for secondary listings and also a placename list for each parish or borough with Trust-owned land**. The Trust also holds protective covenants over several parcels of land in Dorset but these are not listed as the Trust's involvement amounts in practice to a form of planning control and does not have implications for countryside access or the wider public interest.

Inevitably, for reasons of good scenery and efficient management – plus a degree of historical accident – some areas have much more Trust land than others. Around Kingston Lacy, Golden Cap and in some parts of the Isle of Purbeck the properties described have contiguous boundaries. Each entry is then divided once more into its principal strands of interest, with paragraphs in chronological order about its visible history being followed by potted descriptions of the landscape. There is then a short note of how the Trust acquired ownership and at the end of each item information about the location and its access, the parking and paths. There is also a brief note of the general location at the start of each item, together with an Ordnance Survey map reference (to six figures – the first three read west to east on the map's vertical grid; the following three south to north on the horizontal lines).

I am compiling this as a member of the National Trust's ruling council, from 1990, but though I am grateful to the Trust and its staff for considerable help and encouragement, I must emphasise that the book was not commissioned as an official publication. Nor can the National Trust take any responsibility for the views expressed within it; not that there are very many and none that is intended as critical.

The Trust is carrying out an ongoing environmental audit of its properties, reviewing farm and other leases as opportunities arise, and constantly improving the quality of conservation both of landscape and antiquities.

It has also greatly expanded the opportunities for public access on its properties, both informally and with the dedication of additional public rights of way. There have been numerous welcome improvements, which as chairman of the Open Spaces Society I have been delighted to encourage and endorse. This book is intended as a fitting tribute to the Dorset holdings on the eve of the National Trust's 1995 centenary celebrations.

**Abbott Street**, Pamphill – see entry for **Pamphill Antiquities**

**Acton Quarries**, Langton Matravers – see entry for **Seacombe Bottom**

Agglestone – for **The Agglestone**, Studland, see entry for **Studland Heath National Nature Reserve**

**AILWOOD DOWN, NINE BARROW DOWN, and WESTWOOD FARM**
*between Corfe Castle and Studland*                    *SZ 000 814*
*Neolithic long barrow (SY 997 815)*: Mound of chalk, 112 feet long by

forty feet wide, which would have been built to cover collective burials of the Neolithic period, the Late Stone Age, about 3,500 BC. The barrow, aligned as was usual from west to east (the burial end) is beside later round barrows strung along the skyline at the summit of the Purbeck Hills. This is the only long barrow in the Isle of Purbeck.

*Bronze Age round barrows* (*SY 995 816* to *997 815*): The major cemetery of the Purbeck Hills, each mound covering a single burial urn accompanied with aristocratic grave goods and food for the after-life, erected by the Beaker Folk from the Rhine who established the rich warrior-dominated Wessex culture of 2,100 to 1,500 BC.

Actually there are seventeen mounds on Ailwood Down (giving their name to Nine Barrow Down which has shifted eastwards on the map), though most are too slight to count. Only nine are over two feet high.

They are set in a line running for eight hundred feet along the crest of the Purbeck ridge at six hundred feet above sea level. The largest is a hundred feet in diameter and ten feet high, surrounded by a ditch that is still four feet deep.

All received the attention of eighteenth or early nineteenth century barrow diggers – and should have provided above-average plunder – but no record exists.

*Legend:* That they are the graves of nine kings who were killed in battle.

*Landscape:* The Trust owns the hog's back of the central Purbeck Hills, from the southern slope of Rollington Hill eastwards, with a tongue of valley land and small fields extending south to Westwood Farm and Harman's Cross. Ailwood Down is registered common land (CL138, 31.74 hectares).

The dry chalk sides of Ailwood Down and Nine Barrow Down are designated by the Nature Conservancy Council (English Nature) as a site of special scientific interest for negative reasons – the paucity of their flora. This is poor because the escarpment is exposed to the weather and the full scorching heat of the sun.

An area of gorse scrub lies beside the barrow group but much of the top of this steep-sided double escarpment has been ploughed for cereals. The view is extensive, across the heath and Poole Harbour and northward to the hills of Cranborne Chase and central Dorset. The Swanage valley, the limestone plateau of southern Purbeck, and the sea are overlooked from the other side.

*Trust ownership:* 400 acres, part of the Corfe Castle Estate left to the Trust by Ralph Bankes who died in 1981.

*Location and access:* Park in the viewpoint car-park on the Corfe Castle to Studland road, the B3351, half a mile to the west of the Golf Course.

Walk around the first corner in the direction of the Golf Course and then cross over to the gate. A track cut in the hillside leads uphill and then follows the left-hand field boundary to the wood where it bends to the right to ascend the slope of the Purbeck Hills.

At the top you can continue to the middle of the hill and then turn right along it, towards Corfe Castle. The barrow group is a mile from your car.


**Alexander** – for General Officer Commanding-in-Chief of Southern Command **General Harold Alexander** [later first Earl Alexander of Tunis, 1891–1969] see entry for **Studland National Nature Reserve (Project Fougasse)**


*Alexandrovna* shipwreck – see entry for **Belle Vue Cliffs**


**Algardi** – for Italian sculptor **Alessandro Algardi** [1602–54] see entry for **Kingston Lacy House**


**Antony** – the Trust owns a superb Roman carving of **Mark Antony** [Marcus Antonius, ?83–30BC], see entry for **Kingston Lacy House**


**Antrim** – National Trust chairman, the thirteenth **Earl of Antrim** [1911-77], who chaired the Trust from 1966, has his memorial in Dorset, see entry for **Golden Cap**


**Arne** parish – see entries for **Hartland Moor National Nature Reserve, Middlebere Peninsula, Langton Wallis Heath, and Fayle's Tramway**


**Art and antiquities collections** – see entries for **Brownsea Island (St Mary's Church)** and **Kingston Lacy House**

**Askerswell** parish – see entry for **Eggardon Hill**

**Badbury area Bronze Age finds in the British Museum:** The display of British prehistory in the British Museum galleries include Bronze Age urns and food vessels from Straw Barrow and its neighbouring mounds near Badbury Rings. The 1845 excavators also removed a sandstone block carved with daggers and axes.

## BADBURY RINGS, VINDOCLADIA, CRAB FARM ROMAN FORT, STRAW BARROW, KING DOWN, and THE BEECH AVENUE
*north-west of Wimborne*                                            *ST 964 030*

*Badbury Rings causewayed camp (ST 964 029):* Hedge-sized banks in the interior of Badbury Rings, well inside its greater and later encircling fortifications, are the remains of the enclosure of an extensive Neolithic camp dating to between 3,500 and 3,000 BC.

There was a contemporary settlement adjoining, across most of this round dome-shaped hilltop. With the passing of 5,000 years, and the massive subsequent earthworks, only scant and scattered traces survive above ground of these once substantial entrenchments.

*King Down Barrows (ST 980 034):* Two Bronze Age burial mounds, dating to the Wessex culture between 2,100 and 1,600 BC, lie on King Down, a mile north-east of Badbury Rings. They were formerly ploughed to the edge and two others in this cluster were totally eradicated by cultivation.

There is now some grass back on King Down but its 268 acres of registered common land is still under intensive agriculture and a different landscape entirely from its pre-war appearance as an unfenced sheep range. It was put under the plough as a result of wartime agricultural regulations that came into force in 1940. The National Trust has inherited something of a dilemma under its own statutory requirements for the care of common land.

Common land registered unit CL70 (108.50 hectares) extends from the north side of the B3082 at the east end of the Beech Avenue, between Lodge Farm and the Lodge, northwards for nearly two miles. Its far point is where Pamphill public footpath number 26 leaves the Kingston Lacy estate, heading for Witchampton, between the Bradford Barrow and Old Lawn Farm.

Badbury Rings, on the approach from Wimborne: the Avenue of pollarded beeches, planted in 1835, now wind-torn and duplicated by double rows of replacements. Photograph: Colin Graham.

On the south side of King Down Drove, tree clumps on the hillock beside a disused chalk-pit have expanded into a small but dense wood.

*Straw Barrow group (ST 947 031):* Four Bronze Age burial mounds of the warrior-dominated Wessex culture lie to the south of the B3082 about 500 yards south-east from the west end of the Beech Avenue. Two are in the north-west angle that the trackway, Swan Way, makes with the main road. Straw Barrow itself is on the west side of Swan Way, immediately to the north of the cottages, 500 yards from the road.

The fourth mound is on the other side of Swan Way, and crossed by it, just over a hundred yards from the road.

Significantly, one of these barrows yielded three skeletons as its primary burials, fifteen secondary cremations, several food vessels, and a central cairn of stones. One of the boulders was remarkable in being carved with daggers and axes. The excavation took place in 1845 and the finds are in the British Museum. Straw Barrow seems to have been the one with the treasure but there is some doubt about this.

*Barrows south-west of Badbury Rings (ST 958 030):* This is a group of nine Bronze Age burial mounds from the peak warrior aristocracy of prehistoric civilisation, contemporary with the main phase of the building of Stonehenge.

The three large barrows, close to the car-park access from the B3082, were thought to be Roman because of their surrounding banks and proximity to the Roman road. They are set in a line along it. Excavations have shown, however, that they pre-date the road and are of the standard prehistoric type though with the addition of post-Roman ditches and banks.

*Badbury Rings (ST 964 030):* Major multi-vallate Iron Age hill-fort comprising three sets of ramparts and outer ditches. It was built and extended over a considerable period, with the forerunner of the inner bank being dated to about 700 BC, the centre ring to 400 BC, and the outer circle to AD 40.

Slightly oblong in plan, though visibly appearing as circular, the concentric banks enclose about 18 acres of rounded hilltop. The defences would have been palisaded and are engineered for slingstone warfare with the additional height of the inner banks giving the fire-power advantage to the defenders. They would also have had plenty of shot as the hilltop clays of the Reading beds are peppered with a natural

Badbury Rings downland: one of the best preserved of the Trust's collection of Bronze Age burial mounds, this example having been enhanced by a later encircling bank. Photograph: E. Dodshon.

Badbury Rings and Badbury Clump: turn of the twentieth century view, before the interior vegetation spread outwards across the triple ramparts and ditches of the Iron Age hill-fort. Photograph: E. Dodshon.

supply of slingshot pebbles.

The hill-fort has well preserved outworks and entrances. It was a major fortress of the Durotrigic peoples that saw its last warfare in AD 44-45 when Vespasian's Second Legion started the campaign that conquered the West of England for the Roman Empire. Their marching camp is described below [see *Crab Farm*]. Finds of ballista bolts, fired by Roman artillery machines, have come from around the fort and indicate that it was besieged. Spearheads and swords have also been found.

There is no evidence, however, beyond scholarly wishful thinking, to link Badbury Rings with the great victory of the legendary British leader, Arthur. His epic battle of "Mount Badon", which held back the Saxon advance for thirty years, probably took place near Bath.

Two dewponds, restored in 1984 by young people working with the Prince's Trust, date back to prehistoric times and form of the only standing water for a mile and a half.

Bada's Castle, named for a Dark Ages war-leader, has been the name of the fortifications from AD 710 onwards.

*Vindocladia* (*ST 960 029*): Unimproved downland around Badbury Rings covers a major scattering of Roman antiquities and has yielded a considerable quantity of finds.

The visible remains are the roads, which converge from Hamworthy, Dorchester, Hod Hill, Bath, and Salisbury at an important junction in the form of a double triangle between the northern rampart of the hill-fort and the western end of what is now King Down Drove.

Of the roads which can be traced on the ground, the best preserved is a section of Ackling Dyke from the B3082 at its junction with New Road, extending half a mile north-east to the Shapwick-Pamphill parish boundary hedge. This carriageway survives as a bank 35 feet wide and four feet high, flanked by side-banks and ditches 120 feet apart.

Between the entrance to the downland and the Rings stood the small town of Vindocladia which took its name from the fort's "White Ditches". Occasional disturbances have revealed stone walls and finds of beads, late Roman coinage and black-burnished pottery. There were administrative buildings at the north-west edge of the settlement.

*Badbury Warren and Clump* (*ST 964 030*): Mediaeval warreners utilised the ancient defences of Badbury Rings as a stockade for rabbit breeding, a valuable resource following their introduction by the

Normans, until inevitable escapes led to their general mass colonisation of the entire countryside.

Badbury Warren, the name of the hill-fort in the Middle Ages, gave way to Badbury Clump with the planting of the skyline trees on what was open downland until the eighteenth century. These Scots pines were set out as a piece of landscape gardening, with five vistas radiating as grassy glades from a central viewing area. This feature, since infiltrated by hardwoods, was restored in the 1980s and a bronze topograph mounted on a stone plinth. Adjacent concrete footings held the stays of a wartime radio mast, erected on the summit of the hill, at 327 feet above sea level.

*Badbury Rings downland (ST 960 030)*: Relict colonies of chalkland flowers have spread since the National Trust onslaught on the scrub that had engulfed Badbury Rings and much of its immediate surroundings by 1984. Subsequently, ash trees on the ramparts have been cut as they recover to ten feet, and the grazing regime is a flock of Portland sheep from Calke Abbey, the descendants of those said to have been shipwrecked on the Chesil Beach during the Spanish Armada.

Thirty-four pairs of yellowhammers nested on the south side of the hill-fort in 1991 and apparently endorsed the progressive policy of scrub control.

Some 480 workers sweltered in the tropical summer of 1984 to set back the clock, restoring the Rings to its appearance of 1914, and repairing 139 "erosion scars" caused by human feet as well as attacking the natural regeneration.

*Crab Farm Roman Fort (ST 948 023)*: The outline of a Roman Fort, probably used as a temporary marching camp for the siege of Badbury Rings and the subjugation of the other Stour valley forts by the Second Legion in AD 45-45, lies across arable land near Crab Farm. It is on the north side of the land from Badbury Rings to Shapwick, on the west side of Crab Farm about a mile from the Rings.

The camp is of playing-card shape, rectangular with rounded corners, and the long sides are parallel to the road. The banks are ploughed out and the ditches visible only as crop or soil marks. They can in certain conditions be spotted from the road but there is no general access to the site.

*Crab Farm and the Shapwick Monster:* Crab Farm takes its name from the Shapwick Monster that locals wheeled the village elder to identify

Badbury Rings: earthwork repairs, to deep erosion scars etched into the chalk by generations of visitors' feet, were carried out for the National Trust by youngsters from Birmingham in the sweltering summer of 1984. Photograph: The Prince's Trust.

Badbury Rings, entrance to the hill-fort: trackway through the outer Iron Age ditches and banks, leading into the wooded interior. Photograph: Colin Graham.

– he couldn't, and cried out "Wheel-off, wheel-off". It was a crab that had fallen from a fishmonger's cart or emerged from a heap of seaweed that was being used to fertilize the fields. The story was published in a pamphlet, by Buscall Fox, in 1841.

*The Beech Avenue* (boundary of estate at *ST 945 038* to Lodge at *974 021*): Famous avenue of pollarded beech trees planted by William John Bankes in 1835 as an anniversary gift to his mother, which shrouds the B3082 for two miles on the Blandford side of Kingston Lacy Park. "There is one for each day of the year," to quote the guidebooks – but there are two sides to an avenue and one has an extra tree for leap year. In fact the total was 731 trees, of which in 1985 fourteen were young replacements. The mature trees were already noticeably ageing and requiring surgery or substitution when a hurricane came along in January 1990 and downed a total of forty-one.

The National Trust gave up the losing battle of plugging the gaps and instead established two parallel rows of young replacements set back from the original line.

These will be pollarded after fifteen to twenty years' growth, so that they match their predecessors. Coach driver continue to perpetrate the myth that there is a gold sovereign under each of those; Dorset men had a national reputation for being slow in the head but they were never quite that thick.

The new trees do have some decorative metal, in the form of traditional Kingston Lacy-style iron tree guards, with distinctively flared tops, that were made on the estate.

*Landscape:* Rolling chalk downland. Badbury Clump is the dominant feature. It was planted in the middle of Badbury Rings in the eighteenth century as a central clump with five radiating vistas. Botanists have discovered some rare species of sedge, tufts of marshy grasses, at Badbury. With the exception of the turf grazed by Portland sheep around the Rings the land is a prairie. Most of the intensive arable cultivation is for wheat and barley.

*Trust ownership:* 3,695 acres, part of the lands left to the Trust by Ralph Bankes who died in 1981.

*Location and access:* Crossed by the B3082 for two miles. This is the road across the hills from Wimborne to Blandford and it is overlooked by Badbury Rings which has prominent signposts [four miles north-west of Wimborne] and its own downland car-park.

Badbury Rings, dewpond: holding water since prehistoric times, and hearing about it are the Council of the National Trust, when the Dorset hill-fort starred in their 1991 annual visit to see Trust properties at the grassroots. Photograph: Rodney Legg.

There is general access on foot to the open downland but dogs are banned from the fenced enclosure, following numerous attacks on the sheep, and general access is restricted when point-to-point meets are held on the downs. On the other parts of the estate the access is by lanes or public paths.

Baden Powell – for first scout **Lieutenant-General Robert Baden Powell** [later first Baron Baden-Powell, 1857-1941] see entry for **Brownsea Island**

**Ballard Down Obelisk**, Studland – see entry for **Godlingston Manor**

**Ballard Down**, Swanage – see entry for **Whitecliff Farm**

**Bankes Arms Hotel** – see entry for **Studland Village**

Bankes – for **Cornet Bankes VC** [1835-58], the hero of Lucknow's Indian Mutiny siege, see the entry for **Studland Village**. His posthumous Victoria Cross would be awarded by the Queen in person, to Bankes's mother, on a visit to **Kingston Lacy House**.

**'The Bankes Leaf** in the British Library: One of history's lost pages came to light in 1984 among the Bankes estate papers in the boot room at Kingston Lacy House. It was a vellum leaf which had been re-used as the wrapping for a 1585 copy of a Purbeck title deed. This, it transpired, had come from one of the most famous of the pre-Conquest great bibles, assembled on the instructions of the Venerable Bede in about 712. Bede records in his History of the Holy Abbots how he told Ceolfrith to make three such manuscript copies of the bible, one each for his monasteries of Jarrow and Wearmouth – and the third for the Pope.

That copy went with Ceolfrith to Rome in 716, but the abbot died in France and his bible later came into the possession of the monastery of Monte Amiata, near Florence. It was put in the Laurentian Library in that city in 1786 and is known as the Codex Amiatinus.

The two Wearside bibles were considered to be completely lost but in 1909 Canon Greenwell of Durham came across a leaf in a junk shop in Newcastle. His discovery enabled eleven more leaves to be found, re-used as bindings in the muniments at Wollaton Hall, Nottinghamshire. These were acquired by the British Museum in the 1930s.

One of Ceolfrith's Wearside bibles was stripped apart at Wollaton in the early 1580s, being used for their vellum as folders for copies of title deeds and other legal documents. These transcripts were made in 1585 when Sir Christopher Hatton bought the Wollaton estate from Francis Willoughby.

Hatton, a favourite of Elizabeth I, sat in Parliament for Northamptonshire, though he was losing the queen's attentions in 1584. She had given him Corfe Castle in 1575 and the page from the bible – now known as the Bankes Leaf – was used to bind one of the copies of the deeds relating to the Purbeck estate. By 1585 Hatton was Elizabeth's key man along all four sides of the square that cornered Elizabeth, Parliament, Mary Queen of Scots and the courts. In 1585, Hatton was rewarded with Northamptonshire lands, acquired Wollaton in Nottingham, and was given the keepership to the royal hunting forest of the Isle of Purbeck.

The page from Ceolfrith's bible was spotted in that neglected deed box at Kingston Lacy by Nicholas Pickwoad, the National Trust's consultant on book conservation, who passed it to John Fuggles, the Trust's libraries adviser. Both realised it was important, though at that time neither realised that they were handling pre-Conquest parchment. The Trust then decided it was of such national significance that it should be kept in the British Library.

Bankes – for a potted biography of the Trust's greatest benefactor **Henry John Ralph Bankes** [1902-81] see the entry for **Kingston Lacy House**

Bankes – for Chief Justice of the Common Pleas **Sir John Bankes** [1589-1644] see entries for **Corfe Castle** and **Kingston Lacy House**

Bankes – for "Brave Dame Mary" **Lady Mary Bankes** [died 1661] see entries for **Corfe Castle** and **Kingston Lacy House**

Bankes – for art connoisseur **William John Bankes** [died 1855] see entry for **Kingston Lacy House**

**Barrows** – entries are listed under **Round barrows** and **Long barrows**

**Barry** – for architect (Sir) **Charles Barry** [1795-1860; knighted 1852] see entry for **Kingston Lacy House**

**Beacons** – see entries for **The Hardy Monument/ Lambert's Castle Hill/ Melbury Beacon/** and **Thorncombe Beacon**

**Bee Garden,** Holt – see entry for **Holt Heath National Nature Reserve**

**The Beech Avenue** – see entry for **Badbury Rings**

## BELLE VUE CLIFFS
*south of Swanage*                                            *SZ 015 770*

*Shipwreck:* The rocks at the foot of this cliff stretch eastward towards Round Down and Anvil Point. They are known, descriptively, as the Ragged Rocks and their most horrific death toll was claimed on 29 April 1882.

The Liverpool sailing ship *Alexandrovna* was washed on to these "broken billows which covered the sea with foam for hundreds of yards from the rocks" and all seventy-seven of her crew drowned. A steamer visit in the sunshine of the following week brought ghouls from Bournemouth and Swanage to witness the scene – naked bodies were visible in various stages of mutilation amongst massive quantities of wreckage.

*Landscape:* These are solid Purbeck stone cliffs, rising instantly to about a hundred and fifty feet, with unspoilt limestone downland at the top. The Purbeck stone is still being worked a short distance inland.

*Trust ownership:* 51 acres, bought in 1976 with a donation from Mr L. Forder in memory of his wife, Mrs E.A.E. Forder.

*Location and access:* Immediately west of the Durlston Country Park. Use its car-park.

Turn south along Swanage seafront for almost as far as you can go. Turn right near the end, up Seymer Road, and then swing leftwards up the hill into Durlston Road. The Country Park car-park is at the end.

Black Ven, Charmouth: inhospitable mud-slides form the backdrop to the holiday beach. Photograph: Colin Graham.

You walk westwards along the coastal path, with your back to the Anvil Point lighthouse, for nearly a mile to the stile in an old stone wall. This is the boundary between Dorset County Council's Country Park and the National Trust's Belle Vue Cliffs holding.

Benson – for bibliophile **William Benson** [1682-1754] see entry for **Brownsea Island**

## BLACK VEN

*immediately west of Charmouth*                                        *SY 356 933*

*Old Lyme Road:* The former main coach-road westward to Lyme Regis from the top end of Charmouth now drops into a chasm just beyond Cliff House. The road was carried off by landslips and the area is known as the Devil's Bellows. An alternative route along the cliff-edge, from Old Lyme Hill and Foxley Ridge, suffered the same fate and became part of the undercliff in 1969.

*The Devil's Bellows:* The history of this fast moving cliff-side has been shaped by the mudslides of the Devil's Bellows. The notable landslips of the twentieth century were in the 1920s, 1938, 1957-58 and 1969-70. One witness to the events of 1958 watched trees marching down the cliff on the crest of a mountain of debris that slid out into the sea.

*The name:* Ven is from 'fen', the Old English for a bog. Initial 'f' sounds were pronounced as 'v' in the Dorset dialect.

*Landscape:* This clifftop and undercliff, from 477 feet to sea level, forms the most active landslip in Britain. In 1969 the cliff slid two hundred yards out to sea but these mudflows have since hardened and by 1986 were half eroded by the waves.

The geophysical cause of all this activity is the water from the clifftop ground level, of chert gravels and upper greensand, which permeates to the gault clays which overlie the ammonite beds – reducing the clays to a great ooze of mud. Being unsupported on the seaward side the ground slides in this direction. In between times of slippages the plant life recovers.

Landform geologists study this consolidation which is particularly interesting because of the great tongues of mud that change the tideline. A small bay has developed between them. The cliffs are leased by the National Trust to the Dorset Trust for Nature Conservation.

**Brownsea Island and 'Branksea' Castle:** seen from its private beach, this elegant building is from the outside the creation of Humphrey Sturt in 1765, but conceals an earlier, actual fortress. Photograph: Colin Graham.

*Trust ownership:* 69 acres; 62 acres being bought with Enterprise Neptune funds, 1966-68, and the remainder being a legacy from Miss E.F.R. Nicholls and Miss E.B.I. Nicholls, 1973.

*Location and access:* Car-parks are near the sea in Charmouth, which is a coastal village on the A35 between Lyme Regis and Bridport. Black Ven is immediately south-west of what's left of the Old Lyme Road at the top (west) end of Charmouth. It is only a hundred feet from the nearest buildings in Higher Sea Lane. In 1920 the cliff was twice that distance away.

Drainage schemes may have halted the slippage from above but in parts the undercliff is still moving. It is dangerous to explore a mudflow, so restrict your curiosity to looking down from one of the viewpoints.

**Bond's Folly**, Steeple – see entry for **Creech Grange Arch**

Bradley – for Commander-in-Chief First US Army General **Omar N. Bradley** [1893-1981] see entry for **Old Harry Rocks (Fort Henry)**

**Bramble Bush Bay**, Studland – see entry for **Studland Heath National Nature Reserve**

**Broadwindsor** parish – see entry for **Lewesdon Hill**

## BROWNSEA ISLAND
*in Poole Harbour*                                          *SZ 020 880*

*Roman Pottery (SZ 032 884):* At the north-east corner of the island, 200 feet from the sea wall at the extreme point of the lowest tides, was a Roman pottery kiln. It lies at the extremity of the nature reserve, which has restricted public access. This was one of the Purbeck sites that made black-burnished ware, and perhaps joined with the others in supplying military contracts for the quartermasters of Hadrian's Wall.

*Mediaeval hermitage of St Andrew (SZ 028 876):* Established by the mediaeval monks of Cerne Abbas, apparently in the area of the farm, 150 yards west of the Castle. Seven burials have been dated to between 1100 and 1230. When Colonel William Waugh built the present church in 1835 he took "particular care to preserve the small portion of the chapel wall which remains". If this is incorporated in St Mary's it is well disguised.

Brownsea Island, beneath the pretend 'Castle': this is the real one, the curving walls being the batter of Henry VIII's blockhouse, entombed next to the laundry in the basement of its mock successor. Photograph: Colin Graham.

*Henry VIII's Castle (SZ 031 876)*: Built in 1547, this protected the mouth of Poole Harbour from seaborne attack. It was a square single-storey blockhouse with walls forty feet long and nine feet thick, protected on the three landward sides by a moat and with its hexagonal gun platform facing seaward. Most of its stonework is incorporated in the basement of the present eighteenth century Castle. Queen Elizabeth made a present of the island as a gift for life to "a mere vegetable of the Court, that sprang up in the night", one Sir Christopher Hatton.

*Alum Mines (SZ 021 875)*: Common or potash alum, used medically as an astringent and a styptic, was produced on the southern shore of the island in the area of South Shore Lodge and Barnes' Bottom, with the kilns being on a piece of level ground between the bank and the water. Work in the nineteenth century uncovered old cisterns "formed on solid oak staves". The Mayor of Poole protested to Sir Francis Ashley on 4 February 1586 about the drinking habits of James Mounsey and his men "who farmeth the mines of Brownsea".

*Shelling of the 'Bountiful Gift'*: A case of post-Armada nerves in February 1589 caused the Brownsea garrison to open fire on the copperas-carrying barque *Bountiful Gift* as she attempted to leave Poole Harbour. The master, Walter Merritt, and crewman William Drake were killed. The commander of the castle, Walter Partridge, was convicted of manslaughter but pardoned because he had intended only "to stay the sail ship".

*Civil War preparations:* Four large guns and several chests of muskets were ferried to Brownsea in February 1645 for a twenty-strong Parliamentary garrison.

*Pride's Place:* In the Cromwellian period, in 1645, Colonel Thomas Pride was stationed with the Brownsea garrison. His place in English history is 'Pride's Purge', the forceful exclusion of Presbyterians from their seats in the House of Commons on 3 December 1648. The Brownsea garrison in 1655 captured an intruding vessel which had a commission from James Stuart, the second son of Charles I, who later became James II of England.

*Monmouth interlude:* Charles II and his illegitimate son James Scott, Duke of Monmouth, were rowed around the island on 15 September 1665. They didn't land – because the island was owned by Sir Robert Clayton, to whom Charles owed £30,000. They thought that he too had retreated to the country to escape the plague. Monmouth would return to Dorset, below Ware Cliffs [see its entry], in 1685.

*Seventeenth century mansion:* Little remains of Sir Robert Clayton's large house, which was in ruin by 1800. There are now only two brick walls and piers supporting a gateway, preserved in the courtyard of an old dairy building west of the Castle.

*Copperas manufacture (SZ 021 875):* The sixteenth century alum works was re-opened by Sir Robert Clayton to produce a sulphate of iron, known as green vitriol, that was used in dyeing, tanning and painting. Celia Fiennes, one of the great female explorers, came to Brownsea in 1698-99 and saw the "great furnaces under" that kept the pans boiling, and the adding of old iron and nails.

*Mad Benson's Castle (SZ 031 876):* William Benson bought the island in about 1710 from the executors of Sir Robert Clayton and proceeded to add a "great hall" which transformed the old castle, then still Crown property, into a country house. He grew rare plants in the mild micro-climate, sponsored Samuel Johnson's *Psalms* and erected John Milton's monument in Westminster Abbey. For these he was lampooned by Alexander Pope: "On two unequal crutches propp'd he came, Milton's on this, and on that one Johnson's name ... On poets' tombs see Benson's titles writ." A nervous breakdown followed in 1741, and his love of books turned to hatred. Poole people talked of black masses, necromancy and witchcraft.

*Sturt's Castle (SZ 031 876):* Humphrey Sturt of Crichel House rebuilt the Castle after 1765, into a four-storey tower with wings branching off at all sides. He spent £50,000 on the island. Arthur Young, the agriculturalist who never missed a trick in propagating the virtues of infertile land, credited Sturt with the planting of a million firs [two thousand to the acre, which sounds a little close] and grass that annually improves: "I never have seen finer clover – thicker, more luxuriant, or that promised better to be most profitable land." He concluded that no production could exceed "what may be found in great plenty on this happy island, which is really England in miniature".

*Seymer's House (SZ 018 885):* In ruin on the northern shore; built by Sir Charles Chad who held the island until about 1840. Between it and the mid-northern shore are disused clay-mine shafts and pits.

*St Andrew's Bay, Maryland Village and the Brownsea Pottery episode*

**Brownsea Island, in St Mary's Church: the chapel ceiling dates from 1446 and is from Crosby Place, Bishopsgate, which was the home of Richard III. Photograph: Colin Graham.**

Brownsea Island, in the churchyard: 'This ancient well-head or pozzo surmounts the grave of the late Right Honourable George Augustus Frederick Cavendish Bentinck – brought by him from Italy as a monument of sixteenth century art revival.' Photograph: Colin Graham.

(the Bay is at *SZ 030 880*, the village at *SZ 012 882*, and the Pottery Works at *SZ 013 875*): Colonel William Petrie Waugh bought the island in 1852 and gave £13,000, believing it was worth at least £100,000 an acre "for its clay". It wasn't but as Waugh was a director of the London and Eastern Banking Corporation he had no trouble in raising an instant £237,000 and spent it in 1853-54 on a million bricks to enclose St Andrew's Bay, the embellishment of the Castle, and building himself St Mary's church – by now he needed God on his side. The Lord doesn't suffer fools, however, and the 1855 development of Brownsea [then Branksea] Pottery and Maryland Village for its clayworkers failed to produce Britain's best porcelain and has left us little more than sewer pipes. Thousands of tons of these lie in banks up to eight feet high on the shore opposite the west end of Furzey Island. It is strewn with broken pottery and vitrified bricks for more than four hundred yards. The foundations of Waugh's pottery are in grassland directly opposite the Furzey boathouse. Waugh fled to Spain in 1857 after his deaf wife had received a party of Poole tradesmen who landed to ask if her husband would represent them in Parliament. She responded by asking for time to pay.

*St Mary's Church* (*SZ 028 878*): Brownsea's church stands near the eastern end of the island, at the edge of the woods, and was built by Colonel William Petrie Waugh in 1853-54. The foundation stone was laid in style, watched by a thousand spectators who had been brought across from Poole in a shuttle service of small boats.

It is a pleasant enough piece of Victoriana but the real treasures were imported from London, including the ceiling over the family pew which is said to have come from Crosby Place, Bishopsgate, which was built in 1446. This hall, erected by wool merchant John Crosby, was according to historian John Stow "the highest at that time in London". Later it was the home of Richard III, when he was Duke of Gloucester, and hence the ceiling is a link with the conspiracy to murder the Princes in the Tower. Brownsea's sixteenth century panels also came from London. The pew has a fireplace, eighteenth century candelabrum and a seventeenth century Italian painting of the Crucifixion.

The other Italian objets d'art, include several sixteenth century carvings, among them an ornate, hexagonal pink marble well-head, which is set in the churchyard. They were brought here by George Augustus Cavendish-Bentinck, the owner from 1870 to 1890. The well-head is

**Brownsea Island, southern slopes: 'This Stone commemorates the experimental Camp of 20 boys held on this site from 1st-9th August 1907 by Robert Baden-Powell later Lord Baden-Powell of Gilwell, Founder of the Scout and Guide Movements.' Photograph: Colin Graham.**

above the family grave and surmounted by a wrought-iron canopy with a plaque giving its history: "This ancient well-head or pozzo which surmounts the grave of the late Right Honourable George Augustus Frederick Cavendish-Bentinck – brought by him from Italy as a monument of sixteenth century art revival – has been placed here to his memory by his widow and children."

*Van Raalte effigy:* In mediaeval style, Charles van Raalte [1857-1907] has a superb effigy above his tomb in the family chapel on the south side of St Mary's tower. It was added as a memorial vault in 1908 for the remains of Charles and his devoted Florence who would live another twenty years.

*The Castle fire:* It was gutted on 26 January 1896 whilst the owner, Major Kenneth Balfour MP, was at evensong in the island church. The castle was rebuilt a year later. It now has to be admired from the outside being a holiday home for the John Lewis Partnership and without general public access.

*The island's name – formerly Branksea:* Charles van Raalte, the next owner of Brownsea, was a wealthy socialite who narrowly failed to make it into Parliament as a Unionist [Tory] in then-Liberal Poole. His lasting contribution to the story was to change the island's name, in 1903, from Branksea to Brownsea – which was understandable in the circumstances as his weekend guests had a habit of thinking that Branksome = Branksea [Branksome Station = Brownsea Island]. Constantly having to search the Poole suburbs for upper class waifs and strays to put on the boat decided him upon the change.

*World's first scout camp (SZ 016 876):* The moment of Brownsea's past that is kept alive is the fact that in 1907 Robert Baden Powell chose the south-west side of the island for a camp for twenty boys that was his first outdoor experiment with his ideas on scouting. He divided his boys into patrols and for ten days taught them games and treated them as unarmed combatants – the sort of game that he played in Mafeking as the world watched whilst the Boer War was fought and won in other parts of South Africa. The lads were to be: "Trusty, loyal, helpful, brotherly, courteous, kind, obedient, smiling, thrifty, pure as the rustling wind." One wonders where he found them. Their commemorative stone is on the island's southern ridge, overlooking Furzey Island. Baden Powell was one of the first examples of twentieth century media marketing though his lasting achievement is

**Brownsea Island, east end: neat castellated row of cottages of the eighteenth and mid-nineteenth century, facing the shore and seen from the quay. Photograph: Colin Graham.**

the world scouting movement rather than the Mafeking myth.

*Florence Bonham Christie's secret island:* Enter the dragon, in 1927, with a name sounding like a merger between West End auction rooms. She sacked the loyal van Raalte staff in 1929 and let the island return to nature. Bertha Horthung Olsen threw a visitor in the sea in 1933 and the following year fire devastated all but the eastern end of the island, its smoke clouds reaching France. Peter Scott was declared undesirable; media attention was discouraged and in Poole they talked of spies and rats as big as cats.

*Clearing station for Aliens:* Thousands of Dutch refugees were isolated, questioned and cleared through Brownsea. This armada of small boats put to sea after the Germans smashed into the Low Countries on 10 May 1940 and was shepherded to Brownsea by the Royal Navy.

*1940 Fortifications:* Two six-inch naval guns were mounted on Battery Point, the island's ancient site for a gun emplacement, to guard the entrance to Poole Harbour. The 347th Battery of 554th Coast Regiment of the Royal Artillery proceeded to eat the island's peafowl, reviving a military tradition going back to Alexander the Great.

*Major Strategic Night Decoy, 1941-44 (SZ 012 881):* Rows of large wire baskets, courtesy of the pyrotechnic department at Elstree Studios, were constructed at the west end of the island. They were filled with wood shavings sodden with paraffin and ignited to simulate burning buildings. A bath tub and lavatory cistern flooded them with water to produce a white-hot flash just like a bomb bursting. This drew the German bombers from Poole and Bournemouth. The best documented example was on 22 May 1942 when the initial enemy flares dropped on Poole were extinguished in time for Brownsea to come alive and then rock with countless explosions. In all it saved the Bournemouth conurbation from a thousand tons of German bombs, which is of some personal interest as my parents were among those who would otherwise have received them.

*Post-war obscurity:* Mrs Christie became a total recluse, retreating to a couple of rooms in the Castle, until her death in 1961 at the age of ninety-eight. The time-capsule passed to the National Trust for re-opening to the world.

*Demolition of Maryland Village (SZ 012 882):* Five ruined terraces, each of four pottery workers' cottages, built in 1855 to the north-west of

corner of the island – known as Maryland Village – were demolished by the National Trust in 1963. They had been named for Colonel William Waugh's wife, Mary.

*Dorset Trust for Nature Conservation reserve* (north of a line from *SZ 017 883* to *SZ 032 878*): 200 acres of the northern half of the island has access restricted to small accompanied parties as it is a wildlife refuge. The area is fenced off to the north of the island's main central trackway, Middle Street. Brownsea has one of the last populations of the rare native red squirrel in southern England. About a hundred survive. The heronry above the lake in the centre of the northern woods has around a hundred nests, and is the second largest in Britain. St Andrew's Bay, to the north of the main track from the Castle to the church – an area which Colonel William Waugh temporarily drained in 1853 – now supports one of only three sandwich terneries on the South Coast. The common tern also nests there. More oystercatchers nest on Brownsea than anywhere else in Dorset or Hampshire. Hedgehogs are found on the island and even Sika deer, whose ancestors swam back across from the Rempstone pine forest to re-establish a colony that had been introduced in 1896. Peacock are popular with the visitors, to the extent that notices have been erected asking them to desist from plucking feathers.

*Landscape:* Oval-shaped island with a low sandy ridge along its spine, covered with dense pine woods in the central and northern parts. The hot sandy southern slopes are largely heath and grass. Shallow safe bathing off the south side. I have written a separate descriptive history of the island: *Brownsea: Dorset's Fantasy Island* [1986].

*Trust ownership:* 500 acres, presented to the Treasury by John Bonham Christie, in lieu of estate duties after his grandmother's death on 28 April 1961; handed over to the Trust by the National Land Fund procedure in 1962.

*Location and access:* In the middle of Poole Harbour, served by ferries from Poole Quay and Sandbanks from the start of April to the end of September – or by your own boat to Pottery Pier at the west end of the island. Those arriving by ferry should check the time of the last return boat before they disperse into the island.

Buckman – for geologist **Sidney Savory Buckman** [1860-1919] see entry for **Golden Cap**

Burton Cliff, Burton Bradstock: pea-gravel beach and a sheer cliff of soft, yellow Bridport sand banded with layers of harder stone. Photograph: Colin Graham.

**Burning Cliff** – see entry for **South Down Farm**

## BURTON CLIFF, FRESHWATER, and SOUTHOVER
*at Burton Bradstock*                                    *SY 483 893*

*Smugglers' beacon:* William Crowe's poem *Lewesdon Hill*, of 1788, contains an allusion to "Burton, and thy lofty cliff, where oft the nightly blaze is kindled". A footnote to the first edition explains the reference: "The cliff is among the loftiest of all upon that coast; and smugglers often take advantage of its height for the purpose related in the poem."

*Scam Project:* In the winter of 1943–44 a fleet of Assault Landing Craft came up to the beach and fired batteries of rockets that trailed rope-ladders over Burton Cliff. Troops then landed from another wave of assault vessels and scaled them, in a successful rehearsal for the invasion of Normandy.

*Landscape:* Sheer 100-foot cliffs of yellow Bridport sands, above a wide beach of gritty shingle, with the hilltop pastures slanting inland and views of the Bridport countryside. Burton Cliff is the last green hill between the caravan camps and holiday chalets. There is a path inland from Freshwater to Burton Bradstock along the Trust's bank of the River Bride.

*Trust ownership:* 83.5 acres. The first forty acres were bought in 1967 with Enterprise Neptune funds and a donation from Mrs M.B. Clark. The other land was purchased in 1973 with a bequest from Miss M.A. Jacobsen [via CPRE] and a gift from Miss Edith M. Adlard.

*Location and access:* Off the B3157 Bridport to Weymouth coast road. The Trust's car-park is approached from the Abbotsbury side of Burton Bradstock village. Turn off opposite a thatched cottage [it has the number 93 on its door] and take the road signposted "To beach and car park". Walk down to the beach and turn right. The path climbs Burton Cliff and descends to the River Bride at Freshwater.

**Burton Bradstock** parish – see entry for **Burton Cliff, Freshwater, and Southover**

Castles – see entries for **Brownsea Island (Branksea Castle)/ Corfe Castle/** and **Old Harry Rocks (Studland Castle, lost)**

**Cerne Giant, from the other side of the valley: the 180-feet high chalk-cut hill-figure is generally regarded as a Roman-Celtic version of the god Hercules. Photograph: Colin Graham.**

Cerne Giant, detail: looking skywards up the phallus from between the inner trenches of his legs. Thirty feet in length, the organ became enlarged by the relatively recent incorporation of the navel into the penis. Photograph: Colin Graham.

**Causewayed camp** – see entry for **Badbury Rings (inside the later hill-fort)**

Ceolfrith - for a page from one of the Saxon bibles produced by **Ceolfrith** [642-715] see entry for **'The Bankes Leaf'**

**Cerne Abbas** parish – see entry for **Cerne Giant**

## CERNE GIANT
*at Cerne Abbas*                                          *ST 666 016*

*Hill-figure:* One hundred and eighty feet high outline, said to be of the first century AD, of a naked man brandishing a club that is one hundred and twenty feet long. The trenches that comprise the Giant are no more than two feet wide and are cut into the chalk of a steep hillside overlooking the Cerne valley. The figure has been frequently scoured through the ages, including the period when Cerne was a major Benedictine monastery, to prevent it disappearing under the turf.

This is either a representation of the Roman god Hercules, cut in a native style [the general archaeological opinion] or the Celtic lord of the animals, Cernunnos [the alternative viewpoint]. There was a lion's skin [if Hercules] or serpent [if Cernunnos] draped over the outstretched arm, that was rediscovered in 1979 when Yorkshire Television used a resistivity meter to detect former trenches under the grass.

The nose also survives under the ground, its long parallel sides joined with the eyes like an inverted phallus; it was common in Celtic art for the eyes and nose to be depicted as an upside-down phallus. The Giant's penis is now twenty-two feet in length, because an early twentieth century recutting absorbed the navel into its tip and thereby extended the organ to what is a total of thirty feet if the testicles are included. Phallic representations are common in British Celtic culture and throughout the Roman world. For further information see my own *Cerne Giant and Village Guide* [1990 edition].

*The name:* Cerne, the local river name, is of great antiquity and it is surely more than coincidence that this is the first half of the name of an important Celtic deity. Cernunnos, according to the mediaeval Welsh *Mabinogion,* was the "lord of the wild beasts" – in other words, he was a giant. There is evidence of other lost trenches on the Cerne hillside and these may represent accompanying animals in what was perhaps originally a frieze of Celtic figures.

*Landscape:* The figure is cut into the steep west-facing escarpment of Giant Hill and a block of unspoilt downland rises around it.

*Trust ownership:* Half acre given to the Trust in 1920 by the Pitt-Rivers family and endowed by Sir Henry Hoare in 1924. A further area of hillside was loaned in the 1970s to make the enclosure a manageable size.

*Location and access:* Overlooking the valley road from Dorchester to Sherborne on the northern side of Cerbe Abbas. A public footpath skirts the Giant's enclosure. This path runs northwards from the cemetery at the end of Abbey Street, towards the left hand end of the clump of trees and then uphill, diagonally up the steep slope. There is no access, however, inside the fence; this is a sheep pen.

The figure is clearly visible from a layby, half a mile away beside the valley road, and in a wider panorama from Sydling Hill where the lane to Sydling St Nicholas crosses the next wave of downland.

Champollion – for French Egyptologist **Jean Francois Champollion** [1790-1832] see entry for **Kingston Lacy house (The Philae Needle)**

Charles - for **King Charles I** [1600-49] see entries for **Corfe Castle/ Kingston Lacy House/** and **Winyard's Gap**

**Charmouth** parish – see entry for **Black Ven**

**Chedington** parish – see entry for **Winyard's Gap, Crate's Coppice, Penney's Hill Coppice, White Hill Plantation, and North Hill Plantation**

**Chesil Beach**, Puncknowle – see **West Bexington** entry

**Chideock** parish – see entries for **Seatown, Ridge Cliff, and West Cliff/ Filcombe Farm and Langdon Hall** (listed under **Stanton St Gabriel**)/ **Doghouse Hill** (listed under **Thorncombe Beacon**)

**Chilbridge**, Pamphill – see entry for **Pamphill Antiquities**

Christie – for eccentric **Mrs Florence Bonham Christie** [1863–1961] see entry for **Brownsea Island**

Churchill – for war leader (Sir) **Winston Churchill** [1874-1965] see entry for **Old Harry Rocks (Fort Henry)**

**Clouds Hill**, Turners Puddle – see entry for **Lawrence of Arabia's Cottage**

**Clubmen's Down**, Compton Abbas – see entry for **Fontmell Down**

Coade – for terracotta manufacturer **Eleanore Coade** [died circa 1820] see entry for **Ware Cliffs (Cement Works)**

**Coastal properties** – listed from west to east, see entries for **Ware Cliffs/ The Spittles/ Black Ven/ Stonebarrow Hill/ Stanton St Gabriel/ Golden Cap/ Seatown/ Thorncombe Beacon/ Burton Cliff/ West Bexington/ Portland House (at Weymouth)/ South Down Farm (Ringstead Bay, White Nothe)/ Seacombe Bottom/ Verney Farm/ Belle Vue Cliffs/ Whitecliff Farm/ Old Harry Rocks/ Studland National Nature Reserve/** and **Brownsea Island**

**Colehill** parish – see entry for **Colehill Village Green, Deans Grove, Merry Field Hill, and Leigh Lane**

## COLEHILL VILLAGE GREEN, DEANS GROVE, MERRY FIELD HILL, and LEIGH LANE

*north-east of Wimborne*                      *SU 027 012*

*Colehill Village Green (SU 025 010)*: Crossed by roads at the heart of the village, behind the War Memorial and opposite the distinctive 1893-built tower of St Michael's parish church. This large triangle of once open ground is now virtually climax woodland with dense scrub beneath a canopy of pines. It is a registered village green (VG52).

*Deans Bush (SU 023 013)*: To the north-east of the St Michael's Church, Colehill, this smaller triangle of wild land is a virtual extension of the village green. Its legal status is, however, different as it is registered common land (CL291, 1.54 hectares).

*Merry Field Hill (SU 025 016)*: Most of the north-facing slopes of Colehill, either side of Long Lane and Colehill Lane, are owned by

**Colehill Village Green, near Wimborne: the pines were in their prime soon after the erection of the war memorial in the 1920s. The cross is in Portland stone. Photograph: Rodney Legg collection.**

the Trust. The holding extends for over a mile, from Greenhill to the east of Walford Farm, over Merry Field Hill, to a final field south of Broom Hill. This is still dairying countryside.

*Leigh Lane (SU 028 007)*: Another block of Trust-owned land extends from the trees at the north end of Leigh Lane, southwards to Brookside Farm at the south-east corner of Leigh Common. It is crossed by the track-bed of Castleman's Corkscrew which, in 1846, was the first main-line railway to enter Dorset.

*Landscape:* Ordinary decent southern English countryside, mainly pasture with some attractive thatched cottages and small woods.

*Trust ownership:* 600 acres, part of the lands left to the Trust by Ralph Bankes who died in 1981.

*Location and access:* North-east of Wimborne, either side of Long Lane and Colehill Lane, from Walford and Colehill Village Green to Merry Field Hill, Pilford, and Broom Hill. Mostly tenanted farmland, crossed by a dozen public paths.

**Compton Abbas** parish – see entries for **Compton Down** (listed under **Melbury Beacon**), and **Fontmell Down (Clubmen's Down)**

**Compton Down** - see entry for **Melbury Beacon**

## CONEY'S CASTLE
*north of Charmouth*                                    SY 372 977

*Hill-fort:* Double-banked Iron Age fort of about 400 to 300 BC. It is roughly oval in plan, set north to south on a gravel plateau, with a particularly deep-cut ditch on the east side. Stout ramparts block the northern approaches and outworks were added on the southern side. Unexcavated. Probably pre-dates Pilsdon Pen.

*Name:* The antiquary Charles Warne suggested in 1872 that this derives from 'Cyning', a Saxon king. This is implausible, the obvious one being that coneys were rabbits; Norman warreners who introduced the animal to this country utilised promontories and existing enclosures, like this, to minimise the chances of escape.

*Landscape:* Greensand gravels and chert, formerly quarried in the north-east corner of the fort, which are now largely covered with long grass, foxgloves and scrub. Deciduous woodland is developing in the eastern ditch but the Trust intends to bring this under control. A conifer plantation abuts the north-west side. On the west and east the promontory falls away steeply.

It is over 700 feet high and has views over the Marshwood Vale.

*Trust ownership:* 86 acres, bought in 1975 with a legacy from Mrs (Katharine) Olive Pass of Wootton Manor, Wootton Fitzpaine.

*Location and access:* Turn off the B3165 Lyme Regis to Crewkerne road five miles north of Uplyme – just north of where the really high pylon line, the one with 160-foot towers, crosses the road. Follow this lane to Fishpond and turn uphill in the direction of Wootton Fitzpaine. This byway climbs the spur and runs straight through the middle of the hill-fort. There is a small car-park beside the northern banks.

## CORFE CASTLE
*overlooking Corfe Castle village*                                        *SY 959 823*

*Old Hall:* Herring-bone walling and the windows of a Conquest period hall, on the site of the previous Saxon royal house, pre-dates the rest of the ruins at Corfe Castle. This masonry can be found between the Butavant Tower and the South Tower on the south side of the West Bailey.

*Assassination of Saxon King Edward:* At the entrance to the West Bailey the later South-west Gatehouse [the one beside the Keep] is known as Edward's Gate. Tradition holds that it was built on the spot where seventeen-year-old Edward, King of England, was assassinated by members of his step-mother's household.

Young Edward was the eldest son of Edgar and the natural heir to the throne which he took on his father's death in July 975. On the evening of 18 March 978, after hunting in Purbeck, he called at the *domus* where his stepmother, Elfthryth, and her son Ethelred were living. As he was mounting his horse to leave, Edward was knifed in the stomach, "his bowels being ripped open so as to fall out".

In the words of William of Malmesbury: "The Kinge, findeing himselfe hurt, sett spurs to his horse, thinking to recover his companie; but the wounde being deepe, and fainting through the losse of much blood, he felle from his horse, which dragged him by one stirrop, untill he was left dead at Corfe gate."

The killing was regarded nationally as an outrage. After his body had been removed from Lady St Mary's church at Wareham and taken to

**Corfe Castle, as it was and is: model in a garden behind The Square, showing its pre-1646 profile, with the real thing to the right. Photograph: Colin Graham.**

Shaftesbury Abbey he was elevated to the status of saint and martyr. Miraculous things were claimed.

St Edward's Fountain, a clear trickle issuing from the east edge of the castle hill close to the Wicken Stream, was said to have had healing properties especially powerful in the treatment of failing sight.

*Norman Keep:* The great central keep at Corfe, which despite demolitions still partly stands to eighty feet high, was started about 1095 and completed by around 1105. It is one of the earliest mediaeval fortresses in Britain.

Its general design and style was ahead of its time. It is built upon and otherwise surrounded by an earlier, eleventh century, wall that was about nine feet thick and stood nearly thirty feet high on the outside.

John Hutchins, Dorset's county historian, wrote that, "its structure is so strong, the ascent of the hill on all sides but the south so steep, and the walls so massy and thick, that it must have been one of the most impregnable fortresses in the kingdom before the invention of artillery."

*West Bailey* (around the site of the Old Hall): This was fortified with its three towers in 1201-04, when Corfe Castle was King John's state prison. In 1202 its dungeon held Savaris de Mauléon, a baron from Poitou on the edge of the disputed Aquitaine. He had taken John's mother, Eleanor, prisoner at Vienne. John rescued her.

Of the twenty-five French prisoners held at Corfe "where there was never food nor drink" fifteen starved to death, though Savaris was "turned" as we would say in telespeak – he returned to France as an English agent and became a famous troubadour.

*The Great Ditch:* The deep ditch between the Keep and the vulnerable Outer Bailey was quarried out of the hill in 1207 when John made Corfe his treasury for the store of confiscated church funds and other finances for the coming war against France. A great convoy of carts was needed to move the cash to Portsmouth in 1214.

*King's Hall and John's State Rooms:* Known as the 'Gloriette', these start to the east of the Keep and were built between 1205-08. The east wall stills stands to two storeys and has pointed-arched windows in elaborately mullioned stone. King John enjoyed hunting at Purbeck, where he could also keep an eye on his money.

*Outer Bailey:* Timber palisades around the Outer Bailey were replaced

Corfe Castle: showing, from the Church Knowle road, its commanding strategic position in straddling what became Castle Hill beside the gap in the main range of the Purbeck Hills. Photograph: Colin Graham.

in stone after 1212 but the main perimeter defences date from the second half of the thirteenth century – the First Tower, South-west Gatehouse, Plukenet Tower, Horseshoe Tower, Outer Gatehouse and the Outer Bridge.

*Edward II's imprisonment:* Assassinated King Edward II [1284-1327; reigned from 1307] was held prisoner at Corfe Castle before his murder. One of the prime conspirators was Sir John Maltravers, a knight of the shire of Dorset.

Maltravers had been forced to flee the country after the defeat of Lancaster at the battle of Boroughbridge in 1322. He returned in 1327 to conspire with Edward's wife, Isabella (the daughter of Philip IV of France), to imprison the King. Isabella had a lover, Roger Mortimer, and the trio wanted freedom and power.

Maltravers and his brother-in-law Thomas, Lord Berkeley, deposed the monarch and were paid a hundred shillings a day for holding him at Berkeley Castle, Gloucestershire. The brother seems to have been less determined than Maltravers who, with William Gurney, appears to have murdered Edward in September 1327 while Berkeley was away from his castle. The king was held down on a table and a red hot poker pushed into his anus. In the words of a contemporary chronicler, Higden, he "was sleyne with a hoote broche putt thro the secret place posteriale". His death shrieks were said to have resounded through the castle. Not only had they regarded this as the appropriate method of killing him – revenge for his buggery – but it had the important advantage of leaving no obvious mark. A natural death was claimed and the body put on view to refute suspicions of foul play.

The outcome was that Mortimer and Isabella, now the Queen Mother, ruled the country in the name of the late King's, son Edward III, who was only fifteen-years-old.

Ian McQueen investigated the Dorset link with Maltravers in the Transactions of the Monumental Brass Society for 1966. He writes that Sir John was given the task of inducing the dead King's brother Edmund, Earl of Kent, to plot against the new regime and provide an excuse for Edmund's disposal. This Maltravers achieved by lying to Edmund that Edward was still alive and held at Corfe Castle. It appears that Edward was transferred to Corfe for a short time during his imprisonment and elaborate pretences including an impersonation at a dinner party, were maintained after he had been removed. Edmund fell into the trap and schemed for his brother's escape. He was beheaded.

*Sieges and destruction:* Having survived an abortive siege in 1139 when King Stephen failed to oust one of his barons, Baldwin de Redvers, history caught up with Corfe in the Civil War between King Charles and his Parliament. In 1643, a troop of Parliamentary horsemen tried to use Purbeck's traditional May Day stag hunt as a pretext for entering Corfe Castle.

Lady Mary Bankes had the gates shut against them and until 1646 Corfe was unsuccessfully besieged as the Civil War ebbed and flowed across the English countryside from Marston Moor to Naseby Field. Somerset fell to Sir Thomas Fairfax's cavalry in 1645 and by 1646 the castles at Corfe and Portland were the only token royalist garrisons holed-up in Dorset.

A royalist officer at Corfe, Lieutenant-Colonel Thomas Pittman, conspired to allow a disguised group of the enemy into Corfe. They ended the last forty-eight day siege at 8 am on 27 February 1646 when the Governor, Colonel Henry Anketell, surrendered. His men were caught in impossible crossfire between the intruders inside and the other attackers outside.

On 4 March 1646 the House of Commons ordered the demolition of Corfe, which was no easy task and reducing it to ruins took several months. Some of the undermined masonry slipped down the sides in the subsequent centuries.

*Significance:* Corfe Castle is one of the greatest English castles; even in ruin it remains one of the country's most important historic buildings. Inaccessibility and strength gave it background roles, as a storehouse for treasure, regalia and political prisoners. As a romantic ruin it is spectacular, and since 1958 has been in receipt of government aid to keep it that way.

*Literary associations:* Mary Palgrave was one of five daughters of Sir Reginald Palgrave of Hillside, Peveril Road, Swanage. In *Brave Dame Mary*, published in 1873, she produced a classic and typical Victorian tale with plenty of moral force, describing the heroism of Lady Mary Bankes who defiantly held Corfe Castle against its first Civil War siege in 1643. There is no shortage of condemnation of the Parliamentarians and with this kind of book selling tens of thousands of copies and running into many editions, it is not surprising that we were all conditioned from birth in the righteousness of the royalist cause.

**Corfe Castle: ruined shell of the Keep and slighted outer curtain wall and towers, seen from the adjacent village. Photograph: William Powell.**

*Landscape:* The Castle Hill lies between two streams of the Corfe River, known locally as the Byle and the Wicken, which have cut the only break in the central massif of the Purbeck Hills. The strategic position is superb, commanding the passes on each side, and the visual splendour of the ruins is the equal of anything in Europe. In places the ivy will be retained and gardened by the Trust "to maintain and enhance the romantic quality of the castle". There is a much fuller history of the castle in my book on *Exploring the Heartland of Purbeck* [1986].

*Trust ownership:* 60 acres, being the heart of the Corfe Castle Estate left to the Trust by Ralph Bankes [*see the Kingston Lacy entry*] who died in 1981. It had come into his family in 1635. Corfe Castle was then acquired by Sir John Bankes, the Attorney-General to Charles I, whose wife, Mary, defended it in the Civil War. The Trust's long-term aim with regard to its other properties in Corfe Castle is to acquire ownership over all the properties in The Square but to sell other properties in the village that are surplus to requirements.

*Location and access:* Corfe Castle has been attracting 170,000 visitors a year. The car-park is in the village; turn off the main road into the Square and then left into West Street. The car-park is signposted on the right, after the low terraces of stone-roofed cottages. From March to the end of October the castle is open daily but in the winter months access is restricted to Saturday and Sunday afternoons.

**Corfe Castle** parish – see entries for **Ailwood Down, Nine Barrow Down and Westwood Farm/ Corfe Castle/ Corfe Common, The Rings, West Hawes, and West Hill/ Hartland Moor National Nature Reserve, and New Mills Heath/** and **Scotland Farm**

## CORFE COMMON, THE RINGS, WEST HAWES, and WEST HILL
*south and west of Corfe Castle*                                 *SY 957 817*

*Bronze Age round barrows* (single barrow at *SY 954 824* and a line of them from *SY 956 810* to *966 808*): There is a skyline burial mound at the end of West Hill, with one of the finest views over Corfe Castle ruins and village. The other barrows on the Trust's lands at Corfe Castle are in a line straddling the bracken-covered ridge across the centre of Corfe Common.

Eight, dating from about 2,100 to 1,700 BC, are of varying sizes, from two to eight feet high, and have suffered some disturbance though their contents are unknown.

*Celtic fields (SY 957 808)*: A small group of ancient fields, covering about fifteen acres, lie on the south-facing slope of the western part of the sandy ridge that crosses Corfe Common. Six of these small fields, taking up only two acres, are particularly well preserved. The lynchets, which were cultivation terraces, are about eight feet high.

Though not scientifically dated they are probably prehistoric or Romano-British.

*The Rings (SY 956 820)*: An earthen ring-and-bailey siege work, The Rings was constructed in 1139 by King Stephen, the last of the Norman line. His reign had disintegrated to anarchy and in Dorset he failed to oust Baldwin de Redvers, the first Earl of Devon, from Corfe Castle. The castle stands three hundreds yards to the north-east.

"When traitors perceived that he was a mild man, and soft and good," a chronicler wrote of Stephen, "every powerful man made his castles, and held them against him."

The Rings lie on the first hillock from Corfe Castle, beside the Church Knowle road, and were placed on the side of the slope that tilts away from the Castle Hill – so that the activities of the besiegers were less obvious to watchers on the battlements.

Cromwell's Battery was the name of The Rings until the nineteenth century, because it had been purpose-built for reoccupation by Parliamentary forces for their camp and artillery emplacement in the Civil War of the 1640s. A gun ramp was cut into the north-east side.

*Mediaeval sledge-tracks (SY 958 808)*: Deep cuttings gouged through the sandy ridge at the centre of Corfe Common date from the Middle Ages when sledges laden with marble were hauled across the common from the quarrylands of southern Purbeck. They were destined for the workshops in Corfe village and the export wharf, Ower Quay on Poole Harbour, from which the ecclesiastical building stone and effigies were shipped to London and the country's principal cathedrals and abbeys.

*Lightning strike:* Two cows were struck by lightning and instantaneously killed in a severe thunderstorm on Corfe Common on a September afternoon in 1891.

*West Hawes strip fields and mere-stones (SY 958 817)*: On the west

Corfe Common, south of Corfe Castle: ponies grazing amongst the bracken beneath the Purbeck Hills. Photograph: Colin Graham.

side of the main village car-park at Corfe Castle [off West Street, about midway along] some twenty mediaeval strip fields can be traced in the grass. They are in parallel lines running down the slope to the Corfe River.

The fields are about forty feet wide and up to a hundred and fifty feet long.

Cross into the present fields by the stone stile at the side of the car-park and search out some of the ownership stones – called mere-stones [mere = boundary] – which are like miniature gravestones and carry initials, including "C.C.C.", "N.B." and "R.B."

*Landscape:* Corfe's immediate countryside comprises two very different landscapes. Northwards is the chalk ridge of the Purbeck Hills and to the south the village stretches into the Wealden sands of Corfe Common.

The chalk hills were used for sheep grazing and the indifferent soils to the south for rough grazing for cattle and horses. This is still the case as the bracken-covered marginal land continues to be collectively grazed by those holding rights in common to turn out specified numbers of animals. These are passed on with their properties. Notices point out that non-qualifying stock can be impounded. It is registered common land (CL34, 123.64 hectares, and CL44, 3.60 hectares).

*Trust ownership:* 500 acres, surrounding Corfe Castle village, were left to the Trust by Ralph Bankes who died in 1981.

*Location and access:* Park in the village car-park at Corfe Castle. Turn off the main road into The Square and then left into West Street. The car-park is around the next corner, its entrance is signposted between stone-built houses on the right-hand side, and from it public paths lead northwards and westwards.

These paths lead to West Hawes, The Rings, and West Hill. From the south end of West Street there is a public road and several tracks that fan out across Corfe Common.

**Corscombe** parish – see entry for **Crook Hill**

**Country houses** – only one in the stately home category, see entry for **Kingston Lacy House**, with another grand house being on **Brownsea Island (Branksea Castle)**

**Court House**, Pamphill – see entry for **Cowgrove Common**

## COWGROVE COMMON, MEDIAEVAL MOOT, COURT HOUSE, LOWER DAIRY COTTAGE, WALNUT FARM, and EYE FORD

*north-west of Wimborne*                             *ST 985 000*

*Cowgrove Common (ST 985 000)*: At the west end of the Cowgrove hamlet, a mile from the main road turn-off. First mentioned in 1288, this rustic idyll is a typical piece of mediaeval common land. The common is still at the centre of the community with half-timbered thatched cottages and a traditional farmyard clustered around an open pasture and a duck pond beside the Stour meadows, some of which were named in fourteenth century documents.

*Mediaeval Moot (ST 990 002)*: A rectangular earthwork, 210 feet by 180 feet, cut as platform into the slope above Walnut Farm, the most easterly building on the north side of Cowgrove Lane. It was the meeting place of the manorial court of Kingston and Pamphill, which included the hamlet of Cowgrove. The earthwork is beside the Roman road from Badbury Rings to Hamworthy which would then have still been in use.

A moot was an assembly of local freemen who discussed and organised community affairs – the word survives as a 'moot' point; one that is arguable.

The meeting place continued to function after the Norman conquest, as a mediaeval court leet presided over by the lord of the manor or his bailiff. There are banks three feet high where spectators gathered and the judicial mound a hundred feet across and five feet high which seated the court. Beside this is the execution mound.

The moot is reached through the farmyard gate immediately to the left of Walnut Farm. Ask there if you may see it. Then head to the right, across the field behind the house, to the wooded hedgerow facing you.

*Court House (ST 991 001)*: The most easterly of the Cowgrove buildings, on the south side of the lane, this is also the earliest and preserves the memory of the mediaeval court.

The basic mediaeval fabric is a timber frame that was brick-clad in the seventeenth century. There is an oriel window and others with moulded mullions and leaded lights. Interestingly, like the moot, it lies next to the course of the Roman road – a sign of antiquity – and the later outbuildings have extended across it.

*Lower Diary House* (*ST 991 001*): Immediately west of the Court House, this cottage of the 1600s is of interest for its original and unusual thatched verandah. The cottage was built as a single-storey open hall with an earth floor and a central fireplace. Smoke rose through a slit in the roof.

*Walnut Farm* (*ST 990 001*): The farmhouse is a two-storey seventeenth century thatched building with timber-framed walls. The farms on this part of the Kingston Lacy estate have tree names – Poplar Farm, Firs Farm and Holly Farm.

*Eye Ford* (*ST 996 001*): A wide gravel track, beside a sarsen-stone boulder, leads down to the River Stour from the south side of Cowgrove Lane just over half a mile east of Cowgrove Common, midway between the common and the main road. The hundred foot wide ford and modern wooden footbridge are four hundred yards downstream from where the Roman road from Hamworthy to Badbury Rings crossed the river but they perpetuate the ancient crossing point. You can turn right after you cross the bridge and walk along to the original spot. Eye Ford is the crossing of Eye Mead, meaning 'the island meadow', which is surrounded by arms of the river. It was first mentioned in 1253.

*Landscape:* Leafy lanes and pasture lands on the first fringe of firm ground above the flood plain of the River Stour. The Trust also owns Eye Mead, across the footbridge on the other side of the River Stour, and public access on foot is allowed to these meadows. Traditional agriculture used to encourage their flooding in winter as this prevented the ground freezing and brought on an early crop of grass.

It now provides one of the most delightful riverside strolls in Dorset – marred only by the unfortunate coincidence that it is here the 160 foot high towers of the 400,000 volt national electricity grid, erected in 1960, stride across the valley. They have dwarfed the landscape since Cowgrove and Pamphill lost their screen of the tallest elms in Dorset, to a virulent pandemic of beetle-spread virus in the early 1970s. The hedgerows barely conceal the sliced remains of their giant boles and some I have measured are seven feet in diameter.

*Trust ownership:* 400 acres, part of the lands left to the Trust by Ralph Bankes on his death in 1981.

*Location and access:* Cowgrove Lane is the first turning off the B3082

Cowgrove Common, near Wimborne: duck-pond, mediaeval common land, half-timbered brick and thatch, and Poplar Farm (left, with a roadside Lombardy poplar), beside the Stour meadows. Photograph: Rodney Legg.

Cowgrove Common, to the east of: Court House (left) and Lower Dairy Cottage are among the gems of a remarkable collection of ancient buildings masked as vernacular architecture. Mediaeval timber framing of the Court House was brick-clad in the seventeenth century. Photograph: Colin Graham.

(Blandford) road, opposite the cemetery on the north-west side of Wimborne. Eye Ford is in half a mile and Cowgrove Common is a mile away, with the farms and cottages lying between them.

**Crab Farm** Roman Fort – see entry for **Badbury Rings**

**Crate's Coppice**, Chedington – see entry for **Winyard's Gap**

## CREECH GRANGE ARCH, known locally as BOND'S FOLLY
*near Kimmeridge*                                                    *SY 912 818*

*The physical folly:* An "eye-catcher" designed to appear above the trees of the Great Wood at Creech as a castle silhouetted on the skyline of the Purbeck Hills, when viewed from the Grange country house below. In reverse, from the hill, the view is framed by the stone arch. The single length of wall of grey Purbeck stone is castellated and studded with little pyramids. It was built by Denis Bond, the owner of Creech Grange 1706-46.

*The intellectual folly:* Since I started writing about Purbeck in the Dorset Country Magazine at the end of the 1960s I have done my best to keep alive the local name, Bond's Folly, as it was in danger of being completely eclipsed by the Ordnance Survey's insistence – as a sop to a former landowner of the Grange – on the less revealing "Grange Arch". The reason for the family's embarrassment was that "Bond's Folly" had a double meaning and would originally have been used with a chuckle. For Denis Bond's folly in life was not this arch but the major corruption scandal of the 1720s when he was expelled from the House of Commons, where he sat as a member for Poole, for insider-dealing by "fraudulently and clandestinely" contracting to sell state-owned lands in the Lake District for much less than they were worth.

*Landscape:* Outstanding views from 625 feet, over heathland and the Frome valley; including the reactors of Winfrith atomic research station and the town of Wareham as well as Poole Harbour. The Steeple area is featured in my *Guide to Purbeck Coast and Shipwreck* [1984]; the adjoining army ranges in *Tyneham: Dorset's Ghost Village* [1992]; the clay lands to the north are described in *Purbeck's Heath* [1987].

*Trust ownership:* 1 acre, given by J.W.G. Bond in 1942.

*Location and access:* Four miles south of Wareham. Turn off the A351 at Stoborough, on the road to Kimmeridge. Climb to the top of the Purbeck Hills and park in the Creech picnic area on the brow of the hill. Walk eastwards [away from the army range red flags] for a mile along the prehistoric ridgeway which survives as an attractive green lane along the hog's back of the Purbeck Hills.

## CROOK HILL
*near Halstock*                                                    ST 499 067

*Landscape:* Though only 630 feet high, this minor hilltop lies among the attractive range of wooded slopes along the Dorset–Somerset border to the north of Beaminster. It has views over Halstock and Corscombe, and further into Dorset. In the other direction the hillside falls away and you can see Crewkerne and the Parrett valley.

*Trust ownership:* 6 acres, given in 1965 by R.E. Trevithick.

*Location and access:* Turn east off the A356 Maiden Newton to Crewkerne road at Winyard's Gap. Follow this lane, towards Halstock, for almost a mile. Crook Hill rises on the north side and entails a stiff climb from the roadside.

**Crosby Place** – for part of the ceiling from one of London's grandest houses, sometime home of **Richard III**, see entry for **Brownsea Island (St Mary's Church)**

**Cross-dykes** – see entries for **Fontmell Down** and **Melbury Beacon (Melbury Hill)**

Crowe – for poet **William Crowe** [1745-1829] see entries for **Burton Cliff** and **Lewesdon Hill**

Dempsey – for the Commander of the Second British Army **Lieutenant-General** (Sir) **Miles Dempsey** [1896-1969] see entry for **Old Harry Rocks (Fort Henry)**

**The Devil's Bellows** – see entry for **Black Ven**

Creech Grange Arch, near Wareham: Denis Bond's folly on top of the Purbeck Hills frames a view to the north, over the woods of Creech and heathland of the Army ranges, then across the valley of the River Frome. Photograph: Rodney Legg.

**Devonshire Head**, Lyme Regis – see entry for **Ware Cliffs**

**Dorchester** borough – see entry for **Max Gate**

**Eastington Farm**, Worth Matravers – see entry for **Seacombe Bottom**

Edward – for assassinated Saxon **King Edward** [?963-78] see entry for **Corfe Castle**

Edward – for imprisoned **King Edward II** [1284-1327] see entry for **Corfe Castle**

Edward VII – for **King Edward VII** [1841-1910] see entry for **Kingston Lacy House**

Edward – for the **Prince of Wales**, later **King Edward VIII** [1894-1972] see entries for **Max Gate** and **Godlingston Manor**

## EGGARDON HILL
*north of Askerswell*                                                          *SY 540 946*

*Hill-fort:* Spectacular triple-banked Iron Age hill-fort, dating from 300 BC and given its massive multiple timbered ramparts after 50 BC. The southern half is owned by the National Trust. The north half was ploughed, across the interior and even between the banks on the north side, for crops of kale in the early 1970s; but the Trust's half is undamaged.

The visible concentration of depressions, showing the sites of pits, amounts to a grain capacity on a huge scale and indicates that Eggardon was the economic and administrative hub for the western Dorset chalklands.

The banks of ditches are staggered on the eastern approaches for slingstone warfare (to give the defenders' slings the advantage of height over distance) and to protect the entrance. If after you arrive on the hill you turn to the left and walk the southern ramparts you will find that the central section sags down the hillside – the result of a landslip in antiquity which was remedied by digging a wide ditch in the eastern

**Eggardon Hill, above Askerswell: the Trust-owned southern half of the great Iron Age hill-fort, showing its landslipped ramparts (centre right). Photograph: John White.**

part of the fallen material and reinstating the outer ditch and bank below it.

Inside the earthworks, across ten acres of the southern unploughed interior, are the depressions of some 160 Iron Age pits. Those sampled by excavation were eight feet deep, with the sides cut through the clay-with-flints subsoil. They had been filled with clay. This is unusual; normally at the end of its working life a pit was used as a rubbish tip. At Eggardon they do not seem to have reached this stage. The clay was used as a bung to seal the pits and keep air and rain from the grain.

The pits were therefore awaiting use when the fort was abandoned – indicating that its life was suddenly halted by the Roman invaders before the harvest had been bought in. That would have been the arrival of Vespasian's Second Legion in its three year campaign after the invasion of AD 43.

Eight circles, about thirty feet in diameter, show the sites of huts. Four Romano-British field boundaries also cross the hill, on top of at least one of the prehistoric pits. Says the Royal Commission on Historical Monuments: "With the exception of Hambledon Hill and Hod Hill this appears to be the only large hill-fort in Wessex, and probably the south of England, with extensive visible contemporary remains within it."

*Octagonal sea-mark:* 160 feet across, enclosed by an eighteenth century ditch and bank that cuts through an ancient field bank. Reputedly constructed around a pine-clump planted by the smuggler Isaac Gulliver [1745-1822] who is said to have owned the hill and wanted the trees as a navigation aid. None of the trees survives; there is but one wind-blown hawthorn on the whole of the hill.

*Landscape:* The western escarpment of the Dorset Downs, with outstanding views across the Marshwood Vale and Lyme Regis to Dartmoor and Start Point. Downland turf with bellflowers and butter-flies, including species of the vale as well as the chalk uplands. Wall brown and marbled white mix with painted lady, brown argus, common and chalkhill blue, and four species of skipper. Higher up wheel the buzzards and hawks.

*Trust ownership:* 47 acres, bought from the Fry family in 1978 with vari-ous grants and donations, including a bequest from W.G. Duncombe.

*Location and access:* North of the A35 between Bridport and Dorchester.

Turn off to Askerswell, four miles from Bridport, and take the lane uphill, under the pylon line. Eggardon is entrenched on the skyline to the left of the road.

Eggardon can also be approached from across the downs, from Maiden Newton in the north (via Wynford Eagle) and Winterbourne Abbas to the east. The second route leaves the A35 four miles west of Dorchester and continues straight ahead along the Roman road (ignore the turnings to Compton Valence), passing police radio masts and bringing you to a hilltop crossroads half a mile west of Eggardon.

Park in the layby. Walk southwards a short way, towards Bridport, and then cross the stile on the right-hand side and walk across the earthworks. Keep to the public footpath as you cross the private farmland to approach the hill-fort.

**Egyptology**, Pamphill – see entry for **Kingston Lacy House**

**Eisenhower** – for the Supreme Commander Allied Expeditionary Force **General Dwight D. Eisenhower** [later thirty-fourth President of the United States, 1890-1969] see entry for **Old Harry Rock (Fort Henry)**

**English Nature** – see entries for **Hartland Moor National Nature Reserve/ Holt Heath National Nature Reserve/** and **Studland Heath National Nature Reserve**

**Exercise Smash** – see entry for **Studland Heath National Nature Reserve**

**Eye Ford**, Pamphill – see entry for **Cowgrove Common**

Falkner – for adventure writer **John Meade Falkner** [1858-1932] see entry for **South Down Farm (White Nothe)**

Favenza – for Italian furniture-maker **Vincenzo Favenza** [nineteenth century] see entry for **Kingston Lacy House**

**Fayle's Tramway**, Arne and Corfe Castle – see entry for **Hartland Moor National Nature Reserve**

Fontmell Down, near Shaftesbury: chalkland escarpment dropping into Longcombe Bottom. A beech wood crosses the promontory to the right, above the Blackmore Vale. Photograph: Colin Graham.

Fielding – for novelist **Henry Fielding** [1707-54] see entry for **Winyard's Gap**

**Filcombe Farm**, Chideock – see entry for **Stanton St Gabriel**

**Fishing Barrow Group**, Studland – see entry for **Kingswood Barrows**

Follies – see entries for **Creech Grange Arch** and **Godlingston Manor (Ballard Down Obelisk)**

## FONTMELL DOWN and CLUBMEN'S DOWN
*south-east of Shaftesbury*                                    *ST 887 185*

*Cross-dyke (ST 883 183)*: A shallow ditch and bank, dating from prehistoric times, cuts across the down between the road and the wood. It acted as a defence or a stockade in the Iron Age occupation of the western spur of the down. The promontory it protects, from the Fore Top of Fontmell Down to the slope above Fontmell Magna, is half a mile in length.

*Clubmen's Down (ST 882 184)*: Here, on the open downland west of Gorehedge Corner [Gore Clump], the rector of Compton Abbas, Rev Thomas Bravell, rallied 3,000 men on 25 May 1645. They came from all over Dorset and Wiltshire and moved on to Badbury Rings where, a few days later, "there were present neare 4,000 men armed with swords, bills, pitchforks and several [various] weapons".

Known as the Clubmen of Dorset, because they had initially gathered with clubs, they are said to have been the originators of the word for a collection of people with a shared interest. Theirs was to protest – that the Civil War had dragged on too long, and that both sides should leave them alone.

They presented to King Charles *The Humble Petition of the Distressed Protestants inhabiting the County of Dorset* complaining to have suffered from "these unhappy wars ... in a deeper measure than other of your subjects in this Kingdom" as a consequence "of the many Garrisons in this little County" which remained to be "restored to the blessing of peace". They asked for those who were tired of war to be permitted "to lay down their arms and return to their wonted habitations".

The King was responsive but Sir Thomas Fairfax, replying for the Parliamentary Army, would only promise that "the good discipline of my troops will be maintained".

Three months later, those troops ended the Clubmen's rebellion against "the arbitrary power of the sword" by surprising some 300 of them who were camped on Hambledon Hill, above Child Okeford. It was an unequal contest and twelve Clubmen were killed. The rest were rounded up and herded into Shroton parish church for the night. The following morning they gave assurances that they would disband and were allowed to return to their homes.

*Parish boundary stone (ST 879 182):* Just west of the wood on the Fore Top of Fontmell Down is a small but old parish boundary stone. Compton Abbas [this bit overlooks East Compton] is to the north and Fontmell Magna to the south.

*Landscape:* Close to the roadside entrance to the Trust's downland is one of the classic views of the Blackmore Vale, down the dry Longcombe Bottom – which says just what it is, a long coombe opening into the vale at Fontmell Magna.

The Trust's land is a spur of the chalk escarpment, rising to 750 feet, that marks the western edge of Cranborne Chase. Most of the grass has not been treated with fertilisers and is therefore rich in the typical downland flora that is found on the chalk hills.

Part of the remainder, towards Compton Abbas, has been improved in recent years but will be allowed to revert to natural grassland. The slopes form a superb backdrop to this village.

The southerly coombe has been leased by the National Trust to the Dorset Trust for Nature Conservation.

*Trust ownership:* 282 acres, of which 149 acres were bought in 1977 with local appeal funds and a legacy from Benjamin Meaker. The additional land, the slopes at Gourds Farm on the East Compton side of the hill, was bought in 1982 with a further local appeal that was supported by a Countryside Commission grant.

*Location and access:* On the west side of the Higher Blandford Road, the upper road from Shaftesbury to Blandford, at the top of Spread Eagle Hill which is three miles south of Shaftesbury. There is a small car-park at the top of the hill, overlooking East Compton.

**Fontmell Magna** parish – see entry for **Fontmell Down**

**Fort Henry**, Studland – see entry for **Old Harry Rocks**

**Fowles** – for author **John Fowles** [born 1926] see entry for **Ware Cliffs**

**Freshwater**, Burton Bradstock – see **Burton Cliff** entry

**George** – for **King George VI** [1895-1952] see entry for **Old Harry Rocks (Fort Henry)**

**Godlingston Heath**, Studland – see entry for **Studland Heath National Nature Reserve**

**Godlingston Hill**, Swanage – see entry for **Godlingston Manor**

## GODLINGSTON MANOR, GODLINGSTON HILL, ULWELL GAP, and BALLARD DOWN OBELISK

*between Swanage and Studland*            *SZ 013 810*

*Giants Grave (SZ 012 811), Giant's Trencher (SZ 013 811), and barrow on Godlingston Hill (SZ 014 813), and the Ulwell Barrow (SZ 022 813)*: Despite their 'Giant' names, the first two mounds are low and small, at the head of the dry coombe on the 500 foot contour on the side of Godlingston Hill. They are indeed of note only for their names as the Victorian excavator John Austen opened both in the 1850s but found nothing. The other Godlingston Hill barrow, on the northern spur two hundred yards to the north-east of the named barrows, covered a Bronze Age cremation that was sandwiched between two stones. The six feet high Ulwell Barrow, beneath the obelisk at the west end of Ballard Down, is more interesting, as John Austen dug it in 1857 to reveal a trussed-up skeleton in a chalk-cut grave, with a fine red-ware handled cup which would have held a drink for the journey to the after-world, and an antler in its filling showed how the grave had been dug. There was another, later, skeleton inserted into the mound as well as urn fragments and a cremation beneath a stone. Dated to about 1,800 to 1,500 BC.

**Godlingston Hill and Ballard Down, beside the Ulwell Gap: obelisk, originally a London gas-lamp, erected here to commemorate the abstraction of pure water from the chalk hills for the Victorian town of Swanage (background). Photograph: Colin Graham.**

*Godlingston Manor (SZ 015 803)*: Dating from circa 1300 AD, this privately occupied farmhouse is the oldest inhabited building in Swanage parish, and one of the most ancient in Purbeck. It is at the back of Ulwell – down the western lane [Washpond Lane], four hundred yards beyond the cemetery. A public path runs along its southern frontage. The rounded tower at the west end has walls five feet thick; showing this was the family's fortified refuge as enough remains of contemporary walling to prove that their house had much the same plan as the present manor.

It was in "a sad state of dilapidation" in 1867 and threatened with demolition.

*Literary associations:* Mary Palgrave, the Swanage author of the 1873 Victorian classic *Brave Dame Mary*, set at Corfe Castle, moved the action for its sequel to Godlingston Manor. *Under the Blue Flag* extended the story from 1646 to the Duke of Monmouth's rebellion of 1685.

*Ballard Down Obelisk (SZ 022 813)*: The twenty-three feet high obelisk above the Ulwell Gap on the landward side of Ballard Down is a former London gas-lamp which stood outside the church of St Mary Woolnoth on the corner of King William Street and Lombard Street in the City. It was re-erected here by George Burt in 1892 to commemorate the Swanage Water Act. Water was first tapped from the chalk formation in 1884 and two stone plaques record these events; the reservoir and pumping station are to the south. The white Cornish marble lamp collapsed soon after erection but was rebuilt and next taken down in 1940 when it was regarded as a navigation aid for German bombers. In 1973, through the efforts of Bishop George Snow and the Royal Engineers, it was put back up again though there were difficulties with one six-foot section which had to be left beside the plinth. The gas pipe can be seen running through the centre.

*Godlingston's crash-landing of the Prince of Wales, 1933:* Prince Edward, the playboy Prince of Wales and Britain's once and future king, escaped with his life in 1933 when his plane was forced to crash land in a Dorset field. This incident is one of many from those times which, to the reported "annoyance" of the present royal family was recalled as a result of the Thames Television series *Edward and Mrs Simpson* in 1978. Playing the king, Edward Fox was acclaimed for some of the finest acting ever seen on television.

Four readers of Dorset County Magazine sent me their memories of that nearly fatal day, and below is the most detailed of these, which came from a retired Dorset policeman.

He asked, however, that the magazine should not quote his name: "This issue still raises controversy, though I feel history is eventually going to judge us narrow minded and stupid for losing a strong and thinking monarch who would have lived into the 1970s and brought one of the few stable influences upon the most turbulent and often disastrous years that the world has seen. It heartens me today that the present Prince of Wales models himself in a mild way on Edward VIII, whom he admires as his greatest hero. At least the family can no longer exile its wayward members."

The mishap, and Purbeck's least expected royal visit, took place on 12 July 1933 when the Prince of Wales landed in a cornfield near Godlingston Farm, just below the chalk ridge to the north of Swanage.

The Channel coast was being lashed by a gale and the Prince, after flying over Bournemouth, was heading for Weymouth. Visibility was becoming impossibly poor and the plane was severely bumped by the wind. Luckily, they were over land rather than the bay, and below the clouds there was still some light. It was about 1.15 in the afternoon.

Prince Edward asked the pilot to land in a field. He took his position from the buildings of Swanage Brick and Tile Company, using the chimney stack as a landmark and circling it a couple of times as he descended.

"We thought at first he was going to knock it off," said works director B.P. Codling, referring to the chimney, "but the plane came down nicely in a little wheat field on the other side of the road from here, on land owned by the Bankes estates. The pilot pulled her up by the side of a rick. Afterwards we could find no trace of its descent, the wheat being quite undamaged. Several of us tilers who were near rushed to the assistance of the plane, having seen it in the air, and got the impression it was in difficulties."

The pilot admitted the landing had been far from easy though Prince Edward, with his usual coolness, made light of the whole fuss. He was given a lift to Weymouth by Captain F.R. Bacon of the brickworks. Britain's most fashionable dapper-dresser arrived looking none too spruce, the Bournemouth Daily Echo reported: "His hair was very ruffled and his suede shoes were clogged with mud. His trouser ends were bespattered with mud."

The general opinion was that the Prince had been fortunate to choose the agricultural pocket of the Purbeck Hills for his landing. Had the plane been forced to attempt a landing amongst the miles of heather on the other side of the hill then the results might have been very different.

Three years later the other problem caught up with him. To quote a jingle of 1936:

*A big fast Buick painted black,*
*With Mrs Simpson in the back.*

*Landscape:* The Ulwell Gap is a dry cutting through the chalk ridge of the Purbeck Hills, with steep escarpments rising from two hundred feet to 550 feet on the east side and 654 feet on the west. It is a dramatic landscape with fine views over the Swanage valley to the south and Godlingston Heath, Studland and Poole Harbour to the north. The Trust's lands around Ulwell are featured in my book on *Old Swanage* [1983].

*Trust ownership:* 500 acres, part of the Corfe Castle Estate left to the Trust by Ralph Bankes who died in 1981.

*Location and access:* The Studland and Swanage road passes through the Ulwell Gap and public paths lead off into the hills. Turn off at Ulwell for Godlingston Manor, along either of the lanes that go off to the south-west.

In half a mile you pass Swanage Brick Works, to the right, and then the cemetery on the left-hand side. The next group of buildings, to the right, are Godlingston Manor. There are two dirt tracks on the Swanage side of the farm and both are public footpaths. They take you immediately beside the venerable stone frontage of the manor house, but there is no public access to the interior or elsewhere in the grounds.

**Godlingston Wood**, Swanage – see entry for **Wilkswood Farm**

## GOLDEN CAP
*south-west of Chideock*                                        *SY 407 923*

*Claim to fame:* The highest cliff on the South Coast of England. In excess of Beachy Head, though not as convenient for driving off, its plateau stands at 618 feet above the adjacent sea level, between the valleys of Stanton St Gabriel and Seatown.

**Golden Cap, from Seatown beach: at 618 feet it is the highest cliff on the South Coast of England. Photograph: Colin Graham.**

*Cairns:* Two ancient mounds, probably Bronze Age and covering burials of about 1,600 BC, about four feet high.

*Triangulation pillar:* Erected by the Ordnance Survey, for their instruments.

*Lord Antrim's Memorial:* Block of Purbeck stone with an inset slate plaque, inscribed "Golden Cap. Given by members of the National Trust and friends in memory of the Earl of Antrim KBE, Chairman of the National Trust from 1966 until his death in 1977."

On the back of the boulder, which was brought to the summit in the scoop of a bulldozer in 1978, is a superb fossil cast. Prominent in the upper seaward corner, this was part of the matrix of a big ammonite.

*Ashes of Sidney Savory Buckman:* Lord Antrim's fossil is particularly apposite. For the ashes of Bradford Abbas geologist Sidney Savory Buckman [1860-1929] were scattered from Golden Cap. His pioneering work from the quarries around Sherborne showed how fossils could be used to date the rocks from which they had been taken.

*Landscape:* It is a distinctive cliff with a colourful name that perfectly captures its appearance as the broad band of sand catches the sun.

The flat top is a horizontal mass of chert. Below is the yellow of fine sand, foxmould, which is upper greensand of the Lower Cretaceous period. This contrasts with the underlying dark clays.

An extensive seascape is visible from the top, from Start Point around Lyme Bay to Portland Bill, and there is a breathtaking view down to the inshore waters. Landslipped debris and mudslides have carried a ribbon of rock into the sea. They are known, from east to west, as The Corner, Cann Harbour, The Cove, and the Western Patches. It is classic landform geology.

*Trust ownership:* 26 acres, bought in 1978 in memory of Lord Antrim.

*Location and access:* South of the A35 between Lyme Regis and Bridport. It is an obvious target and you have two parking choices. The easiest walk is from Langdon Wood. For this car-park you turn off the main road between Morcombelake and Chideock, at the top of Chideock Hill, into Muddyford Lane. Then turn immediately left and then right into the trees.

On returning to the main road be careful how you enter the fast traffic on this hill-top dual carriageway.

The other approach is along the coastal footpath from sea level at

**Golden Cap summit: memorial boulder to National Trust chairman the Earl of Antrim, who died in 1977, carried to the top in the scoop of a bulldozer. Photograph: Colin Graham.**

Seatown. For this you turn southwards in the centre of Chideock village, opposite the church, into Sea Hill Lane. There is a non-Trust charge-paying car-park at the end of the road.

**Golden Cap Estate** – see entries for **Golden Cap/ Hardown Hill/ Saint Wite's Well, and Ship Farm/ Seatown, Ridge Cliff, and West Cliff/ The Spittles/ Stanton St Gabriel, Shedbush Farm, Norchard Farm, Filcombe Farm, and Langdon Hill/ Stonebarrow Hill, Cain's Folly, Chardown Hill, Newlands Batch, Westhay Farm, and Upcot Farm/ Thorncombe Beacon, Downhouse Farm, and Doghouse Hill/ Ware Cliffs and Devonshire Head**

Gulliver – for smuggler **Isaac Gulliver** [1745-1822] see entry for **Eggardon Hill**

*Halsewell* shipwreck – see entry for **Seacombe Bottom**

Hamilton – for Scottish aristocrats the **thirteenth Duke of Hamilton** [1862-1940] and the **fourteenth Duke** [1903-73] see entry for **Studland Village (Knoll House grounds)**

**Handfast Point**, Studland – see entry for **Old Harry Rocks**

## HARDOWN HILL
*above Morcombelake*                                    *SY 405 945*

*Barrows:* Seven Bronze Age burial mounds or cairns form a skyline cemetery in the middle of the hill and date from about 2,000 BC.

*Quarries:* The chert deposits were worked for gravel at South Bullen, on the edge of the hill above Morcombelake, and at Johnny Vizer's Pits on the south side of the western spur overlooking Love's Lane and Verriott's Lane.

*Landscape:* Rising to about 650 feet, this great plateau of upper greensand and chert would be stupendous if it were nearer the sea. Instead it is landlocked, a mile from the shore behind the cliffs of Golden Cap and Stonebarrow. Its time has not yet come.

**Hardy Monument, near Portesham: gothic memorial tower to Nelson's flag-captain on HMS Victory, he of 'Kiss me, Hardy', with the foreground seat to Major William Digby Oswald who was killed on the Somme. Photograph: Colin Graham.**

Covered with heather and gorse it is registered common land (CL45, 24.17 hectares).

The western spur is known as The Toyte. 'Tout' was a frequent Dorset name for abrupt coastal hills.

The view seawards is partially blocked by Golden Cap, Stonebarrow and Thorncombe Beacon but inland it is uninterrupted across the Marshwood Vale and brings the Trust's other vale-edge peaks – namely (west to east) Coney's Castle, Lambert's Castle Hill, Pilsdon Pen, Lewesdon Hill and Eggardon Hill.

*Trust ownership:* 25 acres, given by Mrs Angela Scott-Nicholson in 1967.

*Location and access:* Hardown Hill overlooks the A35 Lyme Regis to Bridport road at Morcombelake. It is ascended by several steep footpaths. These lead from the east of the village at Highbullen and Highlands, and from mid-village at Highmead and Caddy Road, as well as Love's Lane. On the north side there are paths from Taylor's Lane and Loscombe's Well Road. The eastern face is climbed from Charleston Corner on the Ryall Road.

## THE HARDY MONUMENT
*north of Portesham*                                        *SY 613 876*

*Napoleonic beacon:* Black Down had an invasion warning beacon at 776 feet, in 1804. This led to the selection of the hilltop for the memorial to Vice-Admiral Sir Thomas Masterman Hardy. Not only was it his local hill, but with the naval success off Cape Trafalgar in October 1805, at which he was Nelson's flag-captain aboard HMS *Victory*, the Royal Navy lifted the eight-year threat of invasion and made its beacon redundant. The next lights along the coast were on Shipton Hill to the north-west and Beacon Hill, now in Puddletown Forest, to the north-east.

*Memorial tower:* Seventy-two feet high, in the shape and style of a Gothic revival factory chimney, which rises from a massive octagonal base with slanting sides that copy the batter of a mediaeval castle. It stands on the top of Black Down and was constructed in grey Portland stone from the Portesham quarries, a mile to the south, which were re-opened for the purpose in 1845-46.

The tower was designed by Arthur Dyke Troyte [according to the Trust's management plan though an earlier document gives Arthur Henry Dyke Acland] and built by Henry Goddard as a sea-mark to commemorate the life of Vice-Admiral Sir Thomas Masterman Hardy who was born at Portesham, the village below the seaward escarpment of the Ridgeway, in 1769. He was Lord Nelson's flag captain aboard HMS *Victory* at the Battle of Trafalgar, 1805, and is remembered as the recipient of that suspect remark from the dying Nelson, "Kiss me, Hardy." Hardy may have misunderstood a Turkish word, "kismet" (then spelt 'kismat') for fate and destiny. Hardy survived the Napoleonic wars and was pensioned off to a shore base, the Navy's Greenwich Hospital, which he governed from 1834 until his death in 1839. He is buried there.

The Hardy Monument cost £605 and was viewed as a job creation scheme in the Hungry Forties. For the celebrations at the laying of the foundation stone, £6 1s 8d was spent on beer and £2 19s 8d for bread and cheese for the work people. The stone was laid by Mrs John Floyer, the wife of the county Member of Parliament.

A stone staircase winds to the top of the tower but has not been open to the public since the 1930s.

*Soldier's seat:* The stone seat on the seaward side of the Hardy Monument is a memorial to Major William Digby Oswald who was killed on the Somme on 16 July 1916, at the age of thirty-six, by the shell-band from a British gun which fired prematurely. Oswald had seen action behind enemy lines and was a veteran of the Boer war, Natal rebellion and Zulu rising. He was buried on the Somme, at Dives Copse near Bray, but his comrades decided upon an English memorial, overlooking the Weymouth countryside where he had met his wife, Catherine Yardley.

*Landscape:* The Ridgeway at the Hardy Monument rises to 784 feet on an isolated pocket of gravel heathland that caps the chalk formation. The view is one of the most famous in southern England, across to Portland and the Chesil Beach and extending to the Isle of Wight on one side and over the sweep of Lyme Bay to Start Point on the other. Inland, you look across the downlands of central Dorset.

*Trust ownership:* ¾ acres, purchased in 1938 with a maintenance fund being established by Sir Robert Williams.

*Location and access:* Visible from great distances. The inland approach is from the A35 Dorchester to Bridport road [turn off at Winterbourne Abbas or via Martinstown].

From the B3157 Weymouth to Bridport coast road you turn off at Portesham and climb steeply uphill. There is a car-park beside the tower.

# HARDY'S COTTAGE BIRTHPLACE

*Higher Bockhampton, east of Dorchester*                    *SY 728 925*

*Literary associations:* The thatched cottage where life began for Thomas Hardy, as a frailty which the nurse thought was dying, on 2 June 1840. This room is upstairs, above the living room, at the north end of the cottage and what became Hardy's own room is above the kitchen with a view from the window seat to the Hardy Monument, the memorial to that "other Hardy".

Thomas was a builder's son who soon found middle class aspirations. He became an architect in Dorchester – the Casterbridge of his novels – before leaving for London where he studied English literature and modern languages at King's College. His first writing was achieved in this cottage, including *Under the Greenwood Tree* [published in 1872]. His first published novel, in 1871, was *Desperate Remedies.*

To Hardy, the cottage was "a little one-eyed blinking sort o' place" and he remembered the foliage closing in on the front door: "The walls of the dwelling were for the most part covered, though these [creepers] were rather beaten back from the doorway – a feature which was worn and scratchy by much passing in and out, giving it the appearance of an old key-hole."

The subsequent course of the author's career is outlined in the entry for Max Gate, which is also owned by the Trust.

*Memorial stone:* Just north of the end wall of the cottage is a memorial, under the trees, erected in 1931 "by a few of his American admirers". When Hardy died, in 1928, his body was cremated – against his wishes – for the supposed honour of a national burial in poet's corner, Westminster Abbey, and his heart alone was put where he wished to lie, in Mellstock churchyard [to use his name for the local parish church at Stinsford].

*Landscape:* This is one of the divides of the Dorset landscape, where the heathland finally gives way to the dominance of the chalk downlands. The last fling of the sandy vegetation is around Rainbarrows, the prehistoric burial mounds on the east side of Thorncombe Wood. The canopy of this old wood overshadows the south side of the cottage and fringes the relict heathland. Eastwards, post-war forestation transformed the previously open view into a dark mass of conifers but by 1986 the Trust had negotiated with the Forestry Commission for the removal of the nearest stands of offending trees.

Hardy's Cottage, near Dorchester: garden view showing rooms where the author Thomas Hardy was born (upstairs, centre window) and wrote his first novel (upstairs, right-hand window). Photograph: Colin Graham.

Hardy's Cottage, south bedroom: Thomas Hardy's bedroom, with a view westwards to his namesake Admiral Hardy's Monument, was where 'Under the Greenwood Tree' was written. Photograph: Colin Graham.

Hardy's Cottage and Max Gate: the Trust owns not only the birthplace of Thomas Hardy but also his main home in nearby Dorchester, where he would die in 1928, having been awarded the Order of Merit and already secure in his reputation as a major English novelist and poet. Photograph: Rodney Legg collection.

*Trust ownership:* 2 acres, the house and an acre being bought in 1948 through the provision of Kate Hardy's will [his sister]; the second acre was bought in 1967 with a legacy from Miss M.M. Groves.

*Location and access:* Turn south off the A35 midway between Dorchester and Puddletown, and then first left [half a mile] into a lane. The car-park is signposted into Thorncombe Wood [owned by Dorset County Council] and there is a track to the cottage through the trees. On a wet day it is easier to walk back along the lane and then turn right and walk the length of the lane through the hamlet of Higher Bockhampton. This is Cherry Lane which used to be called Veterans Valley when it housed the retired survivors of Napoleon's wars. The second gate from the cottage, a little way down the lane, is open to the public from April to October [11 am to 6 pm, or sunset: except Tuesday mornings] and leads to the viewing area in the corner of the garden. Access to the house is by appointment, with the custodian on Dorchester [0305] 62366 or by writing with a stamped addressed envelope to Hardy's Cottage, Higher Bockhampton, Dorchester, Dorset DT2 8QJ.

Hardy – for author **Thomas Hardy** [1840-1928] see the entries for **Hardy's Cottage Birthplace** and **Max Gate**

Hardy – for *Victory* captain **Vice-Admiral Sir Thomas Masterman Hardy** [1769-1839] of "Kiss me, Hardy" fame, see entry for **The Hardy Monument**

## HARTLAND MOOR NATIONAL NATURE RESERVE, MIDDLEBERE PENINSULA, LANGTON WALLIS HEATH, FAYLE'S TRAMWAY, and NEW MILLS HEATH
*between Wareham and Corfe Castle*                          SY 950 850

*Fayle's Tramway* (originally called the New Line, to distinguish it from the previous cart track, *SY 947 833* to *970 865*): Benjamin Fayle laid a horse-drawn tramway – Dorset's first railway – from his clay-pits at Norden across Langton Wallis Heath, and the southern parts of Middlebere Heath and Hartland Moor, to a jetty on an inlet of Poole Harbour 700 yards east of Middlebere Farm. Production rose as a result from 14,500 tons of clay in 1802 to 22,000 tons in 1808: "The clay is conveyed on small carriages with four wheels, carrying two tons each. Three horses draw ten tons to the sea-side three times a day, at the expense of about sixpence dead-weight."

The gently downhill incline is in wide curves through low cuttings. The gauge was 3 feet 9 inches. The rails had an L-shaped flange [nowadays the flange would be on the wheels]. The surviving sleepers at Middlebere weigh about 70 lbs and are 18 inches square and 9 inches deep, being set in two separate rows rather than crossing the trackbed in the normal fashion.

This splendid rarity of industrial technology was completely overlooked by the Royal Commission on Historical Monuments when they surveyed Purbeck. I have provided a full description in my book on *Purbeck Heath* [1987].

*Langton Wallis:* On the southern side of Hartland Moor a wild expanse of drier heathland is registered common land (CL88, 16.00 hectares, and CL139, 0.65 hectares).

*Landscape:* Hartland Moor is Purbeck's giant sponge, an acid bog with tracts of the Dorset heath, *Erica ciliaris* – a bell-heather with rosy-purple flowers in late summer when the moor is relatively dry. In early autumn the brilliant blue flowers are the marsh gentians, *Gentiana pneumonanthe.* All three British species of sundew, *Drosera rotundifolia, D. anglica,* and *D. longifolia* are found on this wet heath. The land dips to the north ending with a peninsula of meadowland that juts as another bog, this time of *Spartina* cord-grass, into the shallows of Poole Harbour.

*Trust ownership:* 900 acres, 640 of which are leased to English Nature [the Nature Conservancy Council] for a National Nature Reserve. This was established in 1954 and extended later. Part of the Corfe Castle Estate left to the Trust by Ralph Bankes on his death in 1981.

*Location and access:* Turn north off the A351 Wareham to Corfe road at the Norden roundabout, half a mile from Corfe Castle. Scotland Farm lies in a mile, a hundred yards from the lane, at a sharp left bend. The road then continues across the northern edge of Hartland Moor but here there is only restricted access. A track on the right, just before the bridge, leads to Middlebere.

Hayter – for portrait painter **Sir George Hayter** [1792-1871] see entry for **Kingston Lacy House**

**Hedbury**, Langton Matravers – see entry for **Seacombe Bottom**

Hartland Moor, near Arne: Purbeck's big bog, extending for a mile into Middlebere Heath and towards the distant ridge of hills. Photograph: Colin Graham.

Hercules – for a chalk-cut figure of the Roman god **Hercules** see entry for the **Cerne Giant**

**Hillbutts**, Pamphill – see entry for **Pamphill Antiquities**

**Hill-forts** – see entries for **Badbury Rings/ Coney's Castle/ Eggardon Hill/ Hod Hill/ Lambert's Castle Hill/ Lewesdon Hill/** and **Pilsdon Pen**

Hobart – for 'Hobart's Funnies' and **Major-General** (Sir) **Percy Hobart** [1885-1957] see entry for **Studland Heath National Nature Reserve (Studland Assault Training Beach)**

Holbein – for German historical painter **Hans Holbein the Elder** [?1464-1524] see entry for **Kingston Lacy House**

**Holt** parish – see entries for **Holt Heath National Nature Reserve/** and **Holt Wood, Holt Forest, Holt Village Green, and God's Blessing Green**

## HOD HILL

*north of Stourpaine*                                    *ST 855 106*

*Iron Age hill-fort:* Major Durotrigic tribal centre – the largest fortified enclosure in Dorset. The top of the hill and much of its southward sloping side are inside a rectangle of double banks and ditches that surround about fifty-five acres.

On the inside, beneath the main rampart, are a series of irregular pits that were dug as quarry ditches rather than a part of the defences. On the outer slope, on three sides, there is a counterscarp bank. There was no need for this additional defensive line on the west side and there just a single rampart was built, because of the precipitous fall of the ground down to the River Stour.

The banks would have been palisaded with timbers and had walk-ways along the top. They were defended with hand-held slingstone catapults. The hill-fort has a sequence of defences on the same alignment, built over a long period, and was taken over after 200 BC by Celtic immigrants from Gaul.

*Iron Age settlement:* Inside the ramparts there was a major hill-top town

Hod Hill, near Blandford: sophisticated banks and ditches of Vespasian's Roman fort (left to right, enclosing the skyline) at their junction with the earlier Durotrigic rampart (above the trees). Photograph: Colin Graham.

with huts and grain stores. Traces survive but only in the south-east corner of the hill which escaped Victorian and Second World War ploughing.

The best of the group of huts is beside the path into the interior of the fort from the southern entrance above Stourpaine village. It lies about a hundred yards from this break in the earthworks and is twenty-five feet in diameter, enclosing a nettle-filled depression. The entrance faces north-east, away from the prevailing wind, and is barely noticeable as a slight dip in the height of the grass.

*Roman Conquest, AD 44-45:* Hod Hill has the rare distinction of having a known rôle in the conquest of south-west England by the Second Legion Augusta, under the command of Vespasian, a year or so after the Claudian invasion of Britain that crossed the Channel in AD 43.

The archaeologist who recovered the moment was Dr [later Sir] Ian Richmond, with a British Museum team, who dug on the hill in 1951-57. He found that the largest hut, presumably that of the chieftain, had a "systematic scatter of iron heads of Roman ballista [machine-fired] bolts". Eleven of these murderous tips were found, each a little under four inches long, with a socket that would have held the wooden shaft "and a solid four-sided head brought to a sharp point and projecting at the base."

The arc of fire was about ten degrees, from a point a short way outside the defences. Sighting shots and 'wides' were also found.

The ballista machine, Richmond calculated, had been mounted on a siege tower that was fifty feet high.

He used the word "Blitzkrieg" and described a vicious assault that had also carried flaming arrows into the thatch of the chief's hut. With that warning the fort must have surrendered as there was no evidence of the sort of general devastation that would have followed from a full legionary onslaught.

*The Roman Fort:* Hod Hill is the only prehistoric fort in Britain that was then to host a permanent Roman garrison. The Second Legion took over its north-west corner for their own fort.

This is 753 feet by 586 feet and could accommodate 918 men [600 legionaries, 234 troopers, 84 grooms] and 252 horses.

There was a 1,900 gallon water cistern cut into the chalk bedrock. The hospital had a hundred beds – which was four times larger than its equivalent in peaceful areas, indicating that the Dorset campaign had met resistance.

What survives for you to see are the delicately engineered banks of the Roman defences on the flat grassy top of the hill. They are deceptively tame, offering the intruder an easy leap and quick run across fifty-five feet of open ground.

Then came the crunch. His next leap would be into a deep ditch in the shadow of the inner wall and beneath the Roman spears. This was a death-trap from which both progress and retreat were impossible.

The ditches are now smooth and rounded but you can find a slight rise in the inner bank a few feet from the neat entrances. These platforms would have carried the Roman machine-gunner, using a large wooden catapult to fire ballista bolts into anything that broke through the gates. The Roman military manual specified the position of these platforms – they are to the left of the notional target, as viewed from inside the fort.

On that side, the rights of the attackers, the enemy would be unshielded – right-handers to the slaughter. That was their weapon hand; shields were carried in the left.

The fort was in use from about 44-45 to 50 AD. Patrols were sent into the densely populated Cranborne Chase grain-lands to oversee the seizure for the State of two thirds of its corn production, which seems to have been the economic penalty for their stubborn resistance.

*The name:* Hod has been its name from before 1302, and may come from the Old English word 'hod' meaning 'hood' – an allusion to its shape – but 'hod' in Welsh has Celtic roots and means 'quiet'.

A second name, 'Lydsbury', was recorded by W. Boyd Dawkins in 1897 and seems to have been applied to the Roman fort alone.

*Landscape:* Unspoilt chalk downland overlooking the River Stour and the Blackmore Vale. It is of high floristic value with many species of orchid (including bee, frog, fragrant, pyramidal, twayblade, common spotted) as well as horseshoe vetch, devil's bit scabious, autumn gentian, and clustered bellflower.

Butterflies are prolific and include the marbled white, marsh fritillary, chalkhill and other blues. Great green bush crickets are found in the small patches of bramble scrub.

Hod Hill exhibit: its best find is this bronze Romano-Celtic skillet-handle featuring a winged hunting god, reputedly Nodons, holding a hare and a club. Note the crane's bill terminals. The object is in the Ashmolean Museum, Oxford. Photograph: Colin Graham.

Part of the hill is leased by the National Trust as a nature reserve to the Dorset Trust for Nature Conservation and the whole hill is designated by the Nature Conservancy for its scientific interest.

*Trust ownership:* 80 acres. Bought in 1984-85 with funds raised by a local appeal and various grants.

*Location and access:* Hod Hill lies three miles north-west of Blandford, on the west side of the valley road to Shaftesbury, to the north of Stourpaine village. This main road is currently the A350 but with road improvements at some future date this designation may be moved to the Higher Blandford Road.

A footpath climbs Hod Hill from Stourpaine village, from Brook Cottage at the north end of Manor Road.

The other approach is from the lane that turns off westwards from the main road a mile north of Stourpaine. It is signposted to Child Okeford. This road enters a cutting and there is a wood on the other side. Park in the layby in the cutting or under the trees. On the left, on the south side of the road, a muddy track leads up to the hunting gate and a stiff climb to the top of the hill. You enter at the corner with the Roman fort. Keep to the footpaths as you approach the hill-fort as these slopes are private farmland.

**Hod Hill exhibits** *in national museums:* The Romano-British displays in the British Museum include the major finds from Hod Hill. The material incorporates the Victorian collection of antiquities from Hod gathered together by Henry Durden of Blandford. In 1951-57 the British Museum carried out its own excavations of the Roman fort in the north-west corner of the Iron Age hill-fort. The finds include spearheads and ballista-bolts, a bronze oil lamp, tinned buckles and a pendant which are inlaid with niello, and brooches. Best of all, however, are the Romano-Celtic skillet-handle and raven-head in the Ashmolean Museum, Oxford.

## HOLT HEATH NATIONAL NATURE RESERVE
*north-east of Wimborne*                                          *SU 058 040*

*Bull Barrow* (*SU 055 050*): Bronze Age burial mound lying on the ridge above the Mannington Brook at the north-east side of Holt Heath. It is a heather-covered sandy mound, about fifty feet in diameter and nearly five feet high, dating from about 1,800 BC.

*Bee Garden* (*SU 058 040*): Rectangular enclosure with banks three feet high that enclose about 90 feet by 75 feet. It is within a group of larger enclosures that covered a hundred acres of Holt Heath.

It may be quite ancient and the apiary that provided its name could have been the later use for which the convenient clearing was put. There was still subsistence farming carried out on the heath until about 1800, mainly from White House Holding; the mud walls from this have since crumbled to almost nothing.

*Landscape:* Extensive area of heather and gorse to the north of Forestry Commission plantations, declared a National Nature Reserve by the Nature Conservancy Council, now English Nature, to provide a continuing northern refuge for the Dartford Warbler and maintain something of the thin corridor of wild lands that still tenuously links the Dorset heaths with those of the New Forest.

Almost all of Holt Heath, except for the Driver's Plantation beside White Sheet Hill, is registered common land (CL21, 423.08 hectares and by far the biggest block of common land in Dorset).

*Trust ownership:* 1,216 acres, part of the lands left to the Trust by Ralph Bankes who died in 1981.

*Location and access:* Holt is signposted eastwards from the B3078 Wimborne to Cranborne road, about a mile north of Wimborne, and you continue on through the village for a further mile. Climb on to the open heathland at Higher Row. The next mile, mainly of unfenced heath with a cluster of cottages in the middle, is Holt Heath. It continues to the Cross Keys and Summerlug Hill in the east.

There are paths across the generally inhospitable terrain and Bull Barrow is towards the north-east and the Bee Garden to the south-west of the central cottages. On the south side, the heath is bounded by the solid green line of the conifers of the Forestry Commission's White Sheet Plantation.


## HOLT WOOD, HOLT FOREST, HOLT VILLAGE GREEN, and GOD'S BLESSING GREEN

*north-east of Wimborne*                                            *SU 040 060*

*Holt Wood (SU 030 060):* Manorial waste of the manor of Holt, which belonged to the manor of Kingston Lacy, where the cottages of the heathcroppers have encroached upon a remnant of common land, a mile east of Hinton Martell. It is now safeguarded as registered land (CL18, 14.07 hectares).

Holt Heath, north of Wimborne: a great tract of heather-clad common land with the
prehistoric Bull Barrow profiled on the skyline (left). Photograph: Colin Graham.

*Holt Forest (SU 039 055)*: This remnant of mediaeval royal hunting ground is the main surviving block of ancient woodland at Holt, though some of it provided fuel and clearings for eighteenth century cottages. It lies a mile north of Holt, on the east side of the lane to Horton, before you reach Holt Wood. It is registered common land (CL19, 69.84 hectares).

*Holt Village Green (SU 029 038)*: A large triangle of sloping grass opposite the school and Vicarage Farm at the centre of this scattered community. The principal botanical interest lies in the boggy area towards the bottom. It is a registered village green (VG6, 1.64 hectares).

*God's Blessing Green (SU 031 032)*: A little piece of roadside grassland, between Colehill and Holt, with the charm of a fine name in a rustic setting. Beside it stands a thatched timber-framed seventeenth century farmhouse. These roadside verges are registered common land (CL80, 1.32 hectares).

*Landscape:* This collection of common land, ranging from roadside grassland to dense woodland, encompasses the surviving remnants of manorial waste in the parish of Holt. They are mediaeval survivors from a way of farming that has gone.

*Trust ownership:* 225 acres, part of the lands left to the Trust by Ralph Bankes who died in 1981.

*Location and access:* Holt is signposted eastwards from the B3078 Wimborne to Cranborne road, about a mile north of Wimborne. God's Blessing Green is half a mile east from the Pig Oak staggered crossroads which you come to a mile from the main road. Holt is a mile further and after the village the lane bends sharply right. You then turn left and explore the lanes, northwards for about a mile, to Holt Forest. Holt Wood is a little further on, to the left.


**Ichthyosaur fossil** – see entry for **Stonebarrow Hill**


John – for **King John** [?1167-1216, reigned from 1199] see entry for **Corfe Castle**


**King Barrow**, Studland – see entry for **Old Harry Rocks**

**King Down** – see entry for **Badbury Rings**

**Kingston Lacy Gardens**, Pamphill – see entry for **Pamphill Antiquities**

## KINGSTON LACY HOUSE, including THE PARK, PHILAE NEEDLE, and other EGYPTOLOGY
*north-west of Wimborne*                                    *ST 980 018*

*Manor House site (ST 980 014)*: The site of the original Kingston Lacy Manor House of 1170 lies under grass in Kingston Lacy Park, on the south side of the drive.

*Kingston Lacy House (ST 978 013)*: Classical three-storey Restoration house, designed by Sir Roger Pratt and built in 1663-65 by Sir Ralph Bankes to replace his mediaeval residence at Corfe which had been demolished in the Civil War, in 1646 [*see its entry*].

In the entrance hall there is a seventeenth century marble bust claimed by the family to be of Sir Ralph's father, Sir John Bankes [1589-1644], with moustache and goatee beard. He is wearing a shirt, tunic and heavy cloak and is placed on an integral plinth. The sculpture is in the baroque style of Alessandro Algardi [1602-54].

There is more Corfe Castle memorabilia. Life-size bronze statues of Sir John and Lady Mary, the heroine of Corfe's two sieges, stand on the stairs and flank their king. Charles I is seated above a superb panel featuring, in bas-relief, the Corfe siege. These statues are by Baron Carlo Marochetti [whose equestrian Richard the Lionheart stands, sword raised, outside Parliament] and were commissioned by William John Bankes in 1853.

Upstairs in the library, are two cases of thirty-one keys from Corfe Castle and in a cabinet in the drawing room is a reminder of the cause for which it was lost. It is an unredeemed "I owe you" from Charles I, dated 18 May 1644, in the troubled nineteenth year of his reign, for £525 "Received of Sir John Bankes, Knight, Chief Justice our Court of Common Pleas at Westminster ... to be imployed for the finding of twentie horse to serve us in our warres".

A number of the paintings were owned by Ralph Bankes before he moved into Kingston Lacy, including that of two Spanish peasant boys eating fruit, after the style of Bartolomé Murillo [1617-82]; it was bought new and belonged to Bankes in 1659.

**Kingston Lacy House, near Wimborne:** three-storey Restoration house, notable as the most important surviving work of Sir Roger Pratt – the first architect to be knighted – but refaced by Charles Barry in 1835. Photograph: Colin Graham.

Kingston Lacy was originally a brick house with Portland stone dressings, around the windows and doors. This structure, however, was considerably altered in the 1780s and then gutted and its exterior refaced in 1835 when William John Bankes commissioned Charles Barry to refurbish the entire building and add a dormered attic. That operation spoilt much of Sir Roger Pratt's work – which was a pity as it is his most important surviving building, and he does have the distinction of having been the first architect to be knighted. The arms on the north front carry the date 1836.

On the other hand, William John Bankes contributed immeasurably to the contents of Kingston Lacy and left it abounding with art treasures. His collection of Egyptology is displayed in the Billiards Room. Some paintings were not simply acquired for the house, those by Sir Peter Lely [1618-80] being traditionally supposed to have been painted here. Most of the smaller paintings are portraits of members of the Bankes family. Massimo Stanzione painted Jerome Bankes [?1636-86] in Naples. He hangs in the library, as does Henry Bankes MP [1758-1835] who was painted in Rome by Pompeo Batoni in 1779, when he was on the grand tour. Van Dyck painted a pair – Lady Borlase (eldest daughter of Sir John Bankes) and her husband, Sir John Borlase. Other painters employed by the family included Dowdney, Jonson, Kneller, Lawrence, Romney, Roper, and Weigall.

The portrait of William John Bankes, in the saloon, is a preliminary sketch by Sir George Hayter [1792-1871] for his giant canvas of the entire Reform Act Parliament of 1833 which hangs in the National Portrait Gallery.

The art collection ranges far from the parochial. The *Judgement of Solomon* by Sebastiano del Piombo [1485-1547] was bought by William John Bankes in Bologna in 1820 as a Giorgione and hangs in the dining room. Others include Holbein's *Sir Thomas More*, Titian's *Venetian Nobleman*, the Genoese *Marches Cateraina Spinola* by Rubens, and *The Holy Family* by Giulio Romano, bought in Spain as a Raphael. There are two giant paintings on the upper staircase, by Frans Snyders [1579-1657]. Both are gory – one of dogs mauling a horse, and the matching one of a bull meeting a similar end. Napoleon had them for while as part of his loot from Madrid.

Twelve gouaches are copies of Roman frescos by the circle of Michelangelo Maestri. Several paintings are by or after Diego Valazquez [1599-1660].

**Kingston Lacy House, entrance hall: dominated by colonial hunting trophies and a baroque bust of 'Sir John Bankes Kt of Corfe Castle, 1589-1644, Lord Chief Justice of England.' The marble is in the style of Alessandro Algardi. Photograph: Colin Graham.**

Kingston Lacy House, holding the stairs: defiant royalist Lady Mary Bankes, with sword and the key to Corfe Castle, in a life-size bronze sculpted by Baron Carlo Marochetti in 1853. Photograph: Colin Graham.

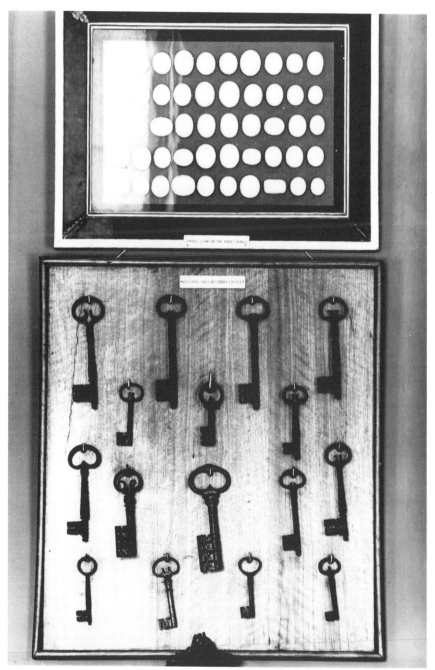

**Kingston Lacy House has the keys of Corfe Castle: two trays, which ceased to be of use in 1646, hang in the Library. 'Impressions of the Pope's rings' are suspended above. Photograph: Colin Graham.**

The Spanish room ceiling is from Venice. The splendid dado is a copy made in 1848 from "scarce old prints" of originals which had perished in the Vatican. The doors are said to have come from the Vatican.

At the top of the staircase the second floor ceiling has an elaborate Italian painting acquired as a Giorgione but this attribution is doubted. It was cleaned from scaffolding during the restoration of the house, 1983-85.

The state bedroom contains a mystery bed, made in the mid-nineteenth century and incomplete when William John Bankes died in 1855. It is a walnut half-tester bedstead with an elaborate headboard carved in relief with Venus, Cupid and putti surmounted by a figure of Motherhood. The tester is supported on caryatids and reeded columns carved with the Bankes arms and some bats. The foot-end has a figure of Silence flanked by angels, and a guardian angel with shields inscribed "Custodit". Its maker was Vincenzo Favenza, whose bills were settled by the British consul on behalf of Bankes's brother, George.

The state bedroom is also out of another century and though the first Bramah water closet was installed in the house in 1785 its plumbing hardly kept pace with the state of the art. Daphne Bankes wrote in 1934: "Without any structural alterations or addition of any disfiguring pipes my mother [Henrietta Jane Bankes] has added for the everlasting comfort of the family and visitors, no less than eight bathrooms. There were no baths at the time of her marriage" [1897]. In many cases she was "cunningly contriving to insert them whenever the experienced brain of the architect had failed to derive means".

Some, however, were so well disguised that the family failed to find them. The window seat in the west bedroom, for instance, was not discovered to be a bath until 1983.

The menfolk of her mother's generation took some pleasure from the colonies, and hunting trophies from Uganda in the 1890s clutter the entrance hall.

There are a few reminders of the last owner, particularly since the touches of homeliness have given way to the illusion of how we think the other half should live. There is a lithography of Henry Ralph Bankes, as a child in 1904, in the state bedroom, and a photograph of him as a lieutenant in the Royal Navy Volunteer Reserve on the deck of HMS *Victory*.

**Kingston Lacy House, the saloon: paintings and finery of the best country house owned by the National Trust in Dorset, and the only one worthy of the stately home category. Photograph: Colin Graham.**

Kingston Lacy House, its art connoisseur: William John Bankes brought home Egyptian treasures and proceeded to enrich the fabric of the house, but would die in exile in Venice. Painted by Sir George Hayter, when Bankes was a member of the Reform Act Parliament of 1832. Photograph: Colin Graham.

**Kingston Lacy Park, the Philae Needle: dated to 150 BC and removed from beside the Nile in 1819. With the Rosetta stone, it was the key to deciphering the hieroglyphs. A conventional nineteenth century obelisk stands in the background. Photograph: Colin Graham.**

*The family scandal:* The art connoisseur William John Bankes was "unusually handsome and was possessed of personal magnetism that captivated men and women alike" – the former causing him particular problems.

In December 1833, when he sat for Dorset in Parliament, he was tried for an indecent act with a soldier in a public lavatory outside Westminster Abbey. He was acquitted after a succession of notable figures testified to his good character, including the Duke of Wellington, Samuel Rogers, and Dr Butler, the master of Harrow.

Then on 3 September 1841 Bankes was committed to the Old Bailey for indecent exposure in Green Park. This time he jumped bail and exiled himself in Venice. He returned sometimes with shipments of art treasures for Kingston Lacy, as far as the family seaboard at Studland, and died in Venice on 17 April 1855.

Parliamentary consent was necessary for the bringing home of his body to the family vault in Wimborne Minster.

*The Philae Needle (ST 979 011):* This ancient Egyptian obelisk, on the lawn south of Kingston Lacy House, was the key that with the Rosetta stone enabled Jean Francois Champollion to decipher the hieroglyphics in 1822.

It is twenty feet high, on a five foot plinth, and stands seventy feet inside from the ha-ha. Lead inscription plaques around the base give the full story:

"William John Bankes Esq MP eldest son of Henry Bankes Esq MP caused this obelisk and the pedestal from which it had fallen to be removed under the direction of G. Belzoni in 1819 from the island of Philae beyond the first cataract and brought this platform" [meaning the stepped base] "from the ruins of Hierassycaminon in Nubia. The granite used in the reparation of this monument was brought from the remains of Leptis Magna in Africa and was given for that purpose by His Majesty King George IV."

"The inscriptions on this obelisk and pedestal record their dedication to King Ptolemy Euergetes II and two Cleopatras his queens who authorised the priest of Isis in the isle of Philae to erect them about 150 years BC as a perpetual memorial of exemption from taxation. This spot was chosen and the first stone of the foundation laid by Arthur, Duke of Wellington August 17 1827."

*Other Egyptology:* Below stairs in Kingston Lacy House is the finest

**Kingston Lacy Park, sarcophagus: the grounds and the Billiards Room have the finest collection of Egyptology that graces any English country house. Photograph: Colin Graham.**

collection of Egyptian antiquities in any country house in the British Isles – not that they were ever appreciated by the Bankes family, other than William John Bankes who collected them on travels up the Nile in 1815-21. In October 1818, on his longest journey, he was accompanied by the British consul, Henry Salt.

Earlier, with Giovanni Finati as his interpreter and guide, he had travelled through the Holy Land and into Syria where, disguised as Bedouin tribesmen, they rode into Petra. Here William made sketches and he also stopped to measure forts, temples and other monuments, to produce the first plans of numerous ruins. Artists were employed to paint watercolours of the sites and terrain and to record ancient wall paintings.

Some of these, as painted plaster panels, he was able to bring home. Six are in the collection at Kingston Lacy and feature dancing girls and a musician. Twenty-five stelae, inscribed memorials, were wall-mounted in the old kitchens. Other items would be literally relegated to the grounds. "A superb striding god was found prone and forgotten in the fernery," the Trust reported in 1992.

The Statuary Workshop repaired that for display and the Billiards Room was chosen for the resurrected display with the billiards table providing an ideal flat, cushioned surface for showing off the wall paintings.

The other special indoor treasure – there are more outside, legitimately in the grounds – is a black basalt Roman head of Mark Antony which was found in Egypt. The Trust has loaned it for exhibition in Oxford and Washington.

*Kingston Lacy Park:* As well as the Philae Needle, the park contains other scatterings of Egyptology including a fine granite sarcophagus which is entombed in a protective box for the winter. An ancient Egyptian lion guards the steps on to the terrace.

Five French mock-cannon of about 1809 are lined up to defend the h-ha, the hidden ditch on the south side of the lawn.

The Portland stone obelisk in the trees (*ST 978 010*) was put up in 1887: "In commemoration of the fiftieth year of the reign of Queen Victoria this monument has been erected by Ralph Bankes on his 34th birthday June 25. Our Empress and Queen was born 1819, crowned 1837, married 1840. Long may she reign." She had visited Kingston Lacy House in 1858 to present a posthumous Victorian Cross to the mother of Cornet Bankes [see *Studland Village entry*].

The specimen trees included "The Royal Tree", a Glaucus Atlas Cedar planted by the King, Edward VII, on 7 December 1905 "in the presence of Mrs Bankes and the tenant, and Henry Ralph Bankes, the son and heir of the late W.R. Bankes". It was blown down in January 1990. A Cedar of Lebanon was planted "by his Imperial Majesty the German Emperor, 8 December 1907". The "Liquidamber" maple was planted by Mary, Princess of Wales [later Queen Mary] on 14 October 1908.

Under the trees is the restored Victorian fern garden with the plants in raised beds. It will be home to a national collection of hardy ferns.

*Stable block* (*ST 977 013*): This beautiful group of buildings, which incorporates the tea rooms, was built by William Ralph Bankes in 1880. The shoes of his favourite racehorses are nailed on a door.

*The name:* 'Kingston' means the 'King's Farm'. From Saxon times until 1603 it was the crux of a huge royal estate which spread even further than today, across 21,000 acres at the time of the Domesday Book, 1086. Lacy was a family name, of owners before the Bankes connection, that of the Earls of Lincoln to whom, William Camden writes in his *Britannia*, "by bargain and sale it came, thro' the hands of Quincie Earl of Winchester, from the Earls of Leicester. For King Henry I gave it to Robert Earl of Mellent and Leicester." In 1603 the estate was given by James I to Sir Charles Bland of Canford as a reward for his efforts in enthusiastically subjugating the Irish.

*Wartime air crash:* DT684, a four-engined Halifax bomber of 58 Squadron from RAF Holmsley South, crashed into the park 300 hundreds north-north-east of Kingston Lacy House (*ST 979 015*) at 13.45 hours on 24 January 1943. Having made two circuits of the aerodrome, on Plain Heath in the New Forest, it was fifteen minutes into a transit flight to Talbenny, Haverfordwest, when the crash occurred.

It had apparently experienced engine failure, losing height over Colehill and then being seen almost touching the tops of the high elms at Chilbridge and Tadden.

The Halifax ploughed into the lawns and trees in front of Kingston Lacy House and broke up on impact. A terrified stag jumped through one of the ground-floor dining room windows.

All the crew were killed. They were Flying Officer M.A. Legg of the Royal New Zealand Air Force (aged 32), Flying Officer G.R. Pringle, a Royal Canadian Air Force air observer (29), and Warrant Officers L.E.

Gilpin (21) and S.J. Prince (25) of the Royal Canadian Air Force, who were wireless operators and gunners.

They are buried in Bransgore churchyard, near Christchurch.

*Restoration work:* The Trust spent £2,000,000 on the extensive restoration programme of 1982-85 which saw massive repairs to the fabric of the house, re-discovery and conservation of its contents, and enrichment of the grounds.

*Bankes family motto: Velle quod vult Deus* [Desire what God wishes].

*Landscape:* There were four avenues into the park, of lime, elm and oak as well as the surviving Beech Avenue. The tree cover is now generally sparse, so many having passed on from maturity, and the Trust began replanting in the mid 1980s. Winds of a hundred miles an hour swept the West Country on the morning of 25 January 1990 and devastated the specimen trees as well as clear-felling swathes through woodland.

Originally, the trees had been planted on a design with diagonal grids and crosses to represent the Union Flag, as is shown on a 1774 drawing by William Woodward.

It was never a spectacular piece of landscaping, though such features as the Snake Pond (*ST 978 017*), dating from Saxon times, would have contributed something. The name derives from 'Snacker' for a decoy pond. In 1986 it was re-lined with clay.

The parkland is flat and grazed by a pedigree herd of sixty Red Devon cattle which were the pride and joy of Ralph Bankes, the last owner. Surplus and lesser specimens go the way of all farm flesh and can be occasionally sampled via Wimborne butchers. Their predecessors were introduced to the park in the early nineteenth century as suckling cows.

*Trust ownership:* 254 acres, left to the Trust by its owner, Ralph Bankes, along with the rest of his estate, on his death in 1981.

*The benefactor:* Barrister Henry John Ralph Bankes [1902-81] was the last private owner of Kingston Lacy House and the 16,000-acre Kingston Lacy and Corfe Castle Estates, which he bequeathed to the National Trust. The Trust's largest ever bequest, it passed into ownership on 19 August 1982, a year to the day after his death.

Ralph Bankes went to Eton and served in the Royal Navy Volunteer Reserve. He became High Sheriff of Dorset [1939]. With the death of his wife, Hilary [1966], he became shy and retiring in his last years at

Kingston Lacy House, the benefactor: last private owner Ralph Bankes, on his death in 1981, left the National Trust its greatest ever bequest – the Kingston Lacy estate and art treasures, plus Corfe Castle, and great sweeps of coast, heath and downland scenery across 16,000 acres of east Dorset. He is seen on HMS Victory in the uniform of the Royal Navy Volunteer Reserve. Photograph: Wright and Logan.

Kingston Lacy; older tenants deny that he was a recluse and resent the implication. "He was a very selfish man but he did the right thing in the end," commented his sister, Mrs Viola Hall.

He is buried towards the top end of Wimborne cemetery.

*Location and access:* Signposted off the B3082, Wimborne to Blandford road, two miles north-west of Wimborne.

There are visiblity splays to the entrance but it is between two bends on a fast stretch of road so be careful in both coming and going. The Trust's car-park is at the side of the house.

Open from April to the end of October, in the afternoons [Saturday through to Wednesday].

## KINGSWOOD BARROWS and FISHING BARROW GROUP on THE ISLE OF PURBECK GOLF COURSE
*west of Studland*          *SZ 007 819* to *018 821*

*Kingswood Barrows* (*SZ 008 820*): Excellently preserved in the field that is reverting to gorseland east of Kingswood Farm, between the B3351 viewpoint layby and the western side of the Isle of Purbeck Golf Club's Trust-owned course.

These four Bronze Age burial mounds are the only collection to survive intact of the scattered groupings along the southern fringes of Godlingston Heath and Studland Heath. They are also the most interesting because three of the mounds are bell barrows, rather than the common bowl type, the difference being an area of untouched flat ground that acted as a berm between the mound and its encircling ditch. The largest of the barrows are those 'bells' closest and furthest from the road. The former is nearly 60 feet in diameter and four feet high with an eight feet wide berm and an encircling ditch about ten feet wide and a foot and a half deep. The other big bell barrow is just over 50 feet in diameter, nearly five feet high, and with a berm fluctuating around 20 feet wide.

This far barrow has had a later but almost contemporary bowl barrow superimposed on the south-south-west side of its 14 foot wide ditch which is otherwise two feet deep. The relationship between the two mounds is probably deliberate and symbolic of family ties. They would each have covered a cremation burial of the warrior Beaker-folk whose Wessex Culture extended between 2,100 and 1,500 BC.

*Thorny Barrow* (site of *SZ 014 821*): I remember this bowl barrow as a substantial mound more than 60 feet diameter and eight feet in height. It is said to have been consumed by a sand-pit. It was of Bronze Age vintage.

*Fishing Barrow Group (SZ 018 821):* The named barrow is the biggest of this otherwise diminutive collection but it has also suffered as a result.

The bell barrow has a sloping berm which gives it an overall diameter of just about 100 feet, plus a ditch 12 feet wide and a foot and a half deep. It is well preserved except for the top, which has been flattened off at a height of nine feet for a golf tee. Enough has been left to dominate the heathland ridge, particularly effectively when there is a golfer on top.

Fishing Barrow takes its name from a well-marked ditch which is waterlogged in winter.

It is another of the rarer 'speciality' burial mounds of the Wessex Culture. The same probably applies to the lesser mounds. Others must remain to be found as I was able to discover two unrecorded specimens further west along this ridge, off the Trust's estate, between Kingswood Farm and Foxground Plantation.

*Landscape:* The barrows are strung out at the foot of the Purbeck Hills along a secondary heathland ridge where the Isle of Purbeck Golf Course makes its encroachments into the heather. They overlook the heath which their makers farmed.

*Trust ownership:* 200 acres, part of the Corfe Castle Estate bequeathed by Ralph Bankes in 1981.

*Location and access:* The Kingswood Barrows are clearly visible if you stop in the viewpoint layby on the north side of the B3351 between Corfe Castle and Studland (*SZ 006 818*). Walk to the east end of the parking area and look down on them.

Fishing Barrow is also conspicuous, rising between Studland public bridleways numbers 25, 26 and 17 only a short distance from the point where they converge. This is on Deans Hill, 300 yards north from where bridleway 25 leaves the B3351 (*SZ 017 819*).

**Knoll House Hotel**, Studland – see entry for **Studland Village**

**Knowlton bell legend** – see entry for **Shapwick Village (White Mill Bridge)**

**Labour-in-Vain Farm**, Puncknowle – see entry for **West Bexington**

**Langdon Hill**, Chideock – see entry for **Stanton St Gabriel**

## LAMBERT'S CASTLE HILL

*north of Lyme Regis*            *SY 370 986*

*Hill-fort:* Single-banked Iron Age hill-fort of about 400 to 300 BC with an outer ditch that is much better preserved than the rampart. Unexcavated, but probably earlier than Pilsdon Pen.

*Beacon:* Mediaeval beacon site; almost certainly.

*Fair and Racecourse:* Annual fair held inside the fort on the Wednesday preceding John the Baptist's day [24 June] from 1709 to 1947. The site of the Fair House is immediately inside the fort entrance, on the right-hand side, and other low earthworks mark the sites of stalls and sheep enclosures.

Horse-races were part of the fair and the racecourse was a circuit of the open hilltop south of the fort. For a time, in the nineteenth century, a second fair was held in September.

*Admiralty Telegraph Station:* On the flat top of the hill-fort, east from the centre at a point 220 metres from the entrance, is a mound which is the site of a shutter-telegraph built by George Roebuck in the winter of 1805-06. The system which crossed Dorset was known as the Plymouth Line. Lookouts used telescopes to watch the next station in each direction, which from here were Toller Down to the east and Dalwood Common in the west. Roebuck's system was built at the height of the Napoleonic wars in the months after the Battle of Trafalgar. A warning of invasion in the West Country could have been transmitted to the Admiralty in Whitehall in about thirty minutes – provided that it happened on a clear day. Often, however, these western hills have their heads in the clouds.

In 1822 the stations were converted to a simpler semaphore system devised by Sir Home Riggs Popham. That would be replaced by the Electric Telegraph in 1847, using Samuel F.B. Morse's code, and these watching posts were then abandoned.

*Artistic associations:* Landscape painter Lucien Pissarro [1863-1944], son of the famous impressionist Camille Pissarro, had a cottage at Fishpond Bottom, Whit[e]church Canonicorum. His work there included scenery which is now National Trust land beside the "Road from the hill, Fishpond" and a "Dorset Garden". James Manson [1879-1945], the director of the Tate Gallery [from 1930] frequently shared Pissarro's rural retreat, on the lip of the Marshwood Vale. They maintained a correspondence for thirty-five years, which survives in its entirety in the Ashmolean Museum, Oxford. "They went painting together whenever they could," his daughter, Mary Manson, told me in 1977.

*Landscape:* The hill rises to 842 feet, with views westwards to Dartmoor and across the Marshwood Vale to the Chesil Beach and Portland.

There is a typical common land look to the south-western parts of the hill, with unfenced roads, and patches of gorsy heath. Indeed, the hilltop triangle between the roads is registered common land (CL234). It is studded with tussocks of purple moor grass, *Molina caerulea*, and is a piece of relict scenery that has gone from common-place to rarity in the second half of the twentieth century.

To the north-east is the contrasting ecosystem of the most westerly beech wood in Dorset.

*Trust ownership:* 167 acres, given in 1956 by Colonel A.D. Pass.

*Location and access:* Beside the B3165 Lyme Regis to Crewkerne road, five miles north of Uplyme to the north of where the 160-foot high pylons carry the national grid across the road.

The Trust has a car-park to the south of the hill-fort. There is also a layby beside the phone box on the northern slopes and from there you climb up through the trees.


**Langton Matravers** parish – see entries for **Hedbury, Acton Quarries and the Priest's Way** (listed under **Seacombe Bottom**)/ and **Wilkswood Farm, Talbot's Wood, Langton West Wood, and the Wilderness**

**Langton Wallis Heath**, Arne – see entry for **Hartland Moor National Nature Reserve**

**Langton West Wood**, Langton Matravers – see entry for **Wilkswood Farm**

Lawrence of Arabia: Colonel T.E. Lawrence in classic pose, with dagger and robes of a Prince of Mecca. A national hero of the Great War, he was a willing participant in the creation of his own legend – from which he would come to Dorset to escape. Photograph: Rodney Legg collection.

**Lawrence of Arabia's Cottage:** a tiny gamekeeper's home a mile north from Bovington Camp at Clouds Hill, among the oaks and rhododendron scrub of the heathland parish of Turners Puddle. Photograph: Colin Graham.

# LAWRENCE OF ARABIA'S COTTAGE at CLOUDS HILL

*near Bovington Camp*                                    *SY 824 909*

*Gamekeeper's cottage:* Shown as such in the Frampton family's Moreton estate records for 1808, and definitely known as Clouds Hill in Victorian times – Lawrence did not coin the romantic name, as Dorset writers have assumed.

*Lawrence of Arabia:* The hero of the sideshow to a sideshow, as he himself dismissed it. The media used the desert revolt in Palastine to restore the good name of war with excitement, daring, achievement, and chivalry in exotic places that were literally out of earshot of home [gun barrages in the trenches could be heard in the South Coast towns, Bournemouth included].

Colonel Thomas Edward Lawrence was presented to the nation as Lawrence of Arabia; a notion that owed much to his ready adoption of Arab dress and weapons for photographs in the classic Prince of Mecca pose. Later he may have run from the legend but he co-operated to the full in its creation.

Clouds Hill is the memorial to the running away – the refuge he found when under the assumed name of T.E. Shaw he joined the Tank Corps, at Bovington, in 1923. The cottage was his "earthly paradise" and here he looked forward to a "life-time of Sundays". Not that you are to believe that; people like T.E. Lawrence do not live a single Sunday. His was the fast lane, including literally that where his Brough Superior motor-cycle GW 2275 finally took him to oblivion in his forty-seventh year, leaving *The Seven Pillars of Wisdom* [published in 1926] to fuel the perpetual legend.

On 13 May 1935 he biked to Bovington to send a telegram arranging a meeting with the extreme right-wing author Henry Williamson – an indication perhaps that Lawrence was still politically alert and edging towards a position that might have influenced history. Coming home he swerved to miss two errand boys, and possibly a mysterious black car, and came off the road at a point about four hundred yards south of the cottage on the Bovington side of the sign that indicates a 5-mph limit for tanks (*SY 826 905*). He died on 19 May without gaining consciousness, other than to raise one finger in a gesture that might have Arabic significance but in all probability was no more than a final attempt at communication.

Winston Churchill led the funeral procession: "I had hoped to see him quit his retirement and take a commanding part in facing the dangers which now threaten the country."

Lawrence is buried in the cemetery on the eastern approach to Moreton village, under a conventional academia-and-God inscription provided by his mother – straight ahead from the gate, right of centre, second row from the back – but it is at Clouds Hill that he has his own last words. A Greek inscription he put over the door is variously translated as "Why worry" or "Nothing matters".

The house has photographs, memorabilia, a gramophone and horn, and a sleeping bag (a second sleeping bag disappeared with the influx of visitors in the wake of the Panavision film directed by David Lean).

In Lawrence's words, "the cottage is alone in a dip in the moor, very quiet, very lonely, very bare. A mile from camp. Furnished with a bed, a bicycle, three chairs, one hundred books, a gramophone of parts, a table. Many windows, oak-trees, an ilex, birches, firs, rhododendron, laurels, heather. Dorestshire to look at."

The cottage, in the view of his biographer Michael Yardley, "is essential for a glimpse into the man's soul. It perpetuates the spirit of Lawrence himself."

For further information also see my own book on *Lawrence of Arabia in Dorset* [1988].

*Landscape:* Clouds Hill is a rhododendron smothered knoll on the northern ridge of the east Dorset heathlands. There is just a glimpse of the southward view across the Frome Valley.

*Trust ownership:* Seven and a half acres, given to the Trust in 1937, by A.W. Lawrence, the Colonel's brother. The cottage opposite, occupied by the first caretakers [Pat and Joyce Knowles] was bought in 1957.

*Location and access:* A mile north of Bovington Camp, on the east side of the road just before you reach the junction with the road from Waddock Cross in the west to Gallows Hill in the east. The Trust's land includes a small car-park. The cottage is open from April to September on Wednesday, Thursday, Friday, Saturday, and Bank Holiday Mondays [2 to 5 pm]. From October to March it opens on Sunday only [1 to 4 pm]. "No photography" says the sign. At least, for Lawrence, there is some freedom at last following the fiftieth anniversary of his death as his published works are now in the public domain and free of copyright.

Lawrence – for national hero **Colonel Thomas Edward Lawrence** [1888-1935] see entries for **Lawrence of Arabia's Cottage** and **Max Gate**

Lawrence – for Peninsular War and Waterloo veteran **Sergeant William Lawrence** [1791-1869] see entry for **Studland Village**

Lely – for Dutch portrait painter **Sir Peter Lely** [1618-80] see entry for **Kingston Lacy House**

## LEWESDON HILL
*near Broadwindsor*                                          ST 437 013

*Hill-fort:* Small early Iron Age single-banked encampment of about 400 to 300 BC; earlier than Pilsdon Pen.

*Name:* 'Leuson' – Saxon personal name.

*Landscape:* High, rounded hill rising to about 900 feet and heavily wooded, with beech. Completely different in character from the other nearby hill, Pilsdon Pen, and hence the saying that was first recorded in 1662, "As much akin as Leuson Hill to Pilsen Pen".

Mariners used to call them the "Cow and Calf" [Lewesdon was the calf]. The hill overlooks the pastoral Marshwood Vale and inland to Devon and Somerset.

*Literary associations:* Inspired the poem that carries its name, *Lewesdon Hill*, a lengthy romantic movement offering of 1788 by William Crowe, the rector of Stoke Abbott. This is a brief extract:

> "Thou nameless rivulett, who from the side
> Of Lewesdon softly welling forth, doth trip
> Adown the valley, wandering sportively.
> Alas, how soon thy little course will end!
> How soon thy infant stream shall lose itself
> In the salt mass of waters, ere it goes.
> No name or greatness.
> Yet if flows along
> Untainted with the commerce of the world,
> Or passing by the noisy haunts of men;
> But through sequestered meads, a little spate,
> Winds frequently, and in its wanton path,
> May cheer some droopy flowers, or minister

Lewesdon Hill, near Beaminster: aerial roots of a beech that corkscrews out of the wooded hilltop immortalised by romantic poet William Crowe. Photograph: Colin Graham.

Of its cool water to the thirsty lamb:
Then falls into the ravenous sea, as pure
As when it issued from its native hill."

*Mineral waters:* The water from these hills has been bottled and sold under the name "Lewesdon Spring". In 1985 it was the brand available in the House of Commons cafeterias.

*Trust ownership:* 27 acres, given in 1943 by Colonel R.P.J. Mitchell.

*Location and access:* On the west side of the B3162 Bridport to Broadwindsor road, a mile south-east of Broadwindsor. It is a half mile walk and climb westward along a track from the cottages at Stoke Knap.

Parking here is not easy, because it is a junction on a narrow bend. It would be sensible to turn off east, and drop down into Stoke Abbott which is a mile away. Walk back to Stoke Knap and cross the main road to the double-hedged track on the opposite side.

**Limekiln Hill**, Puncknowle – see entry for **West Bexington**

**Little Sea**, Studland – see entry for **Studland Heath National Nature Reserve**

## LODGE FARM
*north-west of Wimborne*                                    *ST 974 021*

*Lodge Farm:* Restoration and research since Stephen Burden took over this dilapidated farmhouse in 1977 have revealed that it was the pivotal building of the mediaeval Kingston Lacy estate. It was built as a first-floor great hall and solar, with a magnificent oak screen between them, perhaps for John of Gaunt, in the late fourteenth century.

This was a hunting lodge, both for the adjoining 300-acre deer park at Kingston Lacy and a chase which extended for twenty-one miles and was six miles wide. The house was semi-defensive; secure with high walls of iron-impregnated gritstone from the heath and glazing bars set into traceried windows of Chilmark limestone. These, on the ground floor, had only single lights.

Other discoveries have included earlier foundations and fragments of mediaeval murals. Most of the architectural features of the house had been plastered over or rendered in concrete. There were clues to

Lodge Farm, near Wimborne: warm brown heathstone walls of a mediaeval hunting lodge, built in the fourteenth century as a ground-floor great hall and solar, separated by a magnificent oak screen. Photograph: Colin Graham.

its history, such as chamfered beams, set on stone corbels, and other moulded timbers, but at the time Burden moved in it had slipped in the estate's tenancy roll to the status of surplus cottage and was only one stage away from demolition.

*Landscape:* Leafy, being surrounded by limes and other vegetation at the side of the famous Beech Avenue, on the edge of Kingston Lacy Park. The grass becomes a carpet of snowdrops in February.

*Trust ownership:* 5 acres, being part of the estate left to the Trust by Ralph Bankes who died in 1981.

*Location and access:* On the north side of the Beech Avenue close to its south-east end, set back from Pamphill public footpath number 19 which leaves the B3082 at a strip of grass between Lodge Farm grounds and the southern end of King Down common land. The current tenant of Lodge Farm has been opening it to the public, on his own initiative, but that may not be required of future tenants.

**Long Barrow** – see entry for **Ailwood Down (Nine Barrow Down)**

Loveless – for leader of the "Dorsetshire Labourers" **George Loveless** [1797-1874] see entry for **Tolpuddle Martyrs' Tree**

**Lower Dairy Cottage**, Pamphill – see entry for **Cowgrove Common**

**Lyme Regis** parish – see entries for **Ware Cliffs and Devonshire Head**, and **The Spittles**

**Lyme Volcano** – see entry for **The Spittles**

**Manor Farm**, Studland – see entry for **Old Harry Rocks**

Marochetti – for sculptor **Baron Carlo Marochetti** [1805-67] see entry for **Kingston Lacy House**

**Marshwood** parish – see entry for **Lambert's Castle Hill**

**Max Gate, Dorchester: designed by Thomas Hardy the architect for Hardy the novelist, and where he lived from 1885 until his death in 1928. The commemorative sundial (left side of the corner wall) and conservatory were added later. Photograph: Colin Graham.**

Mauléon – for troubadour and prisoner **Savaris de Mauléon** [twelfth century] see entry for **Corfe Castle**

## MAX GATE
*at Dorchester*                                                    *SY 705 898*

*Thomas Hardy's home:* Victorian villa, set back from the Wareham road out of Dorchester, notable for being Thomas Hardy's home from 29 June 1885 until his death there on 11 January 1928 and unique in that he was the only major English novelist to design the house in which he was to produce most of his work. Its three storeys are the creation of Hardy the architect, his first profession, and here he wrote *The Woodlanders, Tess of the d'Urbervilles, Jude the Obscure*, and most of his poetry. R.L. Stevenson, Lawrence of Arabia, the Powys brothers, Gissing, Kipling, Housman, Yeats, Galsworthy, and the Prince of Wales [Edward VIII] were among his visitors.

Hardy's last photograph was taken at Max Gate on 13 September 1927. He had already been parted from his favourite dog as the memorial in the pets' cemetery beneath the Max Gate trees shows: "The famous dog Wessex. Aug 1913 - 27 Dec 1926. Faithful, unflinching."

Commemorating his master's years here is the sundial, high on the south-east corner of the house: "1885. T.H. 1928."

Hardy's study, however, has been recreated in the Dorset County Museum in Dorchester, and Max Gate is a private house. For a time it had seemed likely to become the principal Hardy shrine, with the Daily News considering in 1929 that "there can be no more fitting memorial than this house" and suggesting Mrs Hardy "would readily agree to the suggestion".

Florence Hardy continued to live there and it was not until 1940, after her death, that Max Gate was left to the National Trust by Hardy's sister, Kate, "to retain the same in the present condition as far as possible". At that time the house was requisitioned by the RAF's commander of Warmwell Aerodrome, which fielded Dorset's two front-line Spitfire squadrons in the Battle of Britain.

The Trust has used its rental income as an endowment towards the upkeep of the Hardy Birthplace but the question of a Max Gate museum has been periodically raised, if only by the present writer. For further information see this author's *Literary Dorset* [1990].

*The name:* Mack's Gate was a turnpike toll-bar and gatekeeper's house on the other side of Alington Avenue, facing its junction with Syward Road, was demolished many years ago. Hardy, as always, adopted the local name and gave it a classier spelling.

*Landscape:* Grounds now well-wooded with the trees Hardy planted – privacy was under threat even then. The house sits well amongst its lawns. It was considered ugly when Victoriana was out of fashion but now finds admirers.

*Trust ownership:* 2 acres, being 1.5 acres bequeathed to the Trust by Kate Hardy in 1940, and a 1/2-acre plot to the north acquired in 1966.

*Location and access:* Max Gate stands in trees behind a brick wall on the north side of Alington Avenue and the Wareham road out of Dorchester – the town's A352 approach road – immediately west of the corner with Syward Road. On the other side its boundary now coincides with the massive cutting of the A35 Dorchester by-pass which was gouged out of the chalk in 1988. Opening it on 17 October that year, Roads Minister Peter Bottomley MP said that some of the embankments and cuttings had been specially shaped to retain the views from Maiden Castle and Thomas Hardy's house at Max Gate. Neither the house nor the grounds are open to the public but they can be glimpsed from the highway, between the Trumpet Major public house [another Hardy association, though modern] and the turning to West Stafford.

**Mediaeval Moot**, Pamphill – see entry for **Cowgrove Common**

**Melbury Abbas** parish – see entry for **Melbury Beacon, Melbury Hill, Compton Down, Spread Eagle Hill, and Melbury Down**

## MELBURY BEACON, MELBURY HILL, COMPTON DOWN, SPREAD EAGLE HILL, AND MELBURY DOWN

*south-east of Shaftesbury*                    *ST 870 193 to 915 199*

*Bronze Age round barrows (ST 873 197 and 898 188):* Two bowl barrow burial mounds, dating from about 2,000 BC, are in quite different locations. One is on the summit of Melbury Beacon and the other on the southern slope of Melbury Down, on the north side of Compton Abbas Airfield.

*Iron Age cross-dyke (ST 878 197 to 877 953):* Running for some 300 yards at the 600 feet contour across the central spur of Melbury Hill.

Intended to protect the summit area from attack along its only flat approach, from the east, this earthwork has a ditch which is up to 16 feet wide and five feet deep, rising into an inner bank 20 feet across and eight feet high. There is a 30 yard gap, apparently original, at the centre and this break was subsequently adopted for the parish boundary between Melbury Abbas and Compton Abbas.

*Romano-British ranch boundary (ST 871 201 to 855 195)*: Later than the cross-dyke, because it cuts across it, a substantial ditch runs for a mile along the northern slopes of Melbury Hill. It is clearly visible as it climbs across the open downland from West Melbury to Spread Eagle Hill. It appears to have been an earthwork for keeping stock from straying off the uplands, or being rustled into the forests below. An alternative theory of a "Saxon hollow-way" is unlikely in that it has been engineered and built as a continuous unbroken earthwork, which would have been unnecessary if its sole purpose was for use as a track.

*Celtic field traces:* Only patches survive, with a few low scarps, of a system that in Iron Age or Romano-British times extended over across several hundred acres. The extant traces are north of Compton Abbas Airfield, on Compton Down, and on the northern sides of Clubmen's Down and Fontmell Down. The rest of the system has been eradicated by ploughing and, southwards, by forestry.

*Mediaeval strip-lynchets:* Ancient cultivation terraces, long ago having reverted to sheep-walks, are cut into the hillsides of Melbury Down, Compton Down, and Spread Eagle Hill. The steepest terraced escarpment is between Whitehall and Melbury Beacon.

*Melbury Beacon (ST 873 197):* A Spanish Armada beacon-site of 1588, Melbury Beacon was brought back into action as a warning fire-watch in 1804, when French invasion was feared. It would have been alerted to an alarm from the Dorset coast via the strategically placed beacon on the other side of the Blackmore Vale at Bulbarrow Hill. From Melbury the warning would have been relayed to Stourhead and Fonthill in Wiltshire. It was guarded night and day, at a cost to the government of 1s 6d each day, to prevent "the sudden Firing of any of these Beacons (which) would create much Hurry and Confusuon and if done without proper orders would be attended with the most serious consequences". The cost of making Melbury serviceable was £18 18s. There are numerous undulations on the hilltop, among which a series of hollows may be imagined as flues.

Such means of calling an alarm became obsolete in 1805, after the Battle of Trafalgar, with the introduction of the shutter-telegraph developed by George Roebuck [*see entry for Lambert's Castle Hill*].

*Landscape:* Formerly common grazing, these open sheep-leazes rise into one of the finest downland hilltops in Dorset. Melbury Hill lies northern-most at the end of the chalk escarpment that runs from Stourpaine to Cann. The grandeur is increased because it seems almost to stand alone, the 862-feet summit being held by only a long spur to the main uplands of Cranborne Chase. On the other side, westwards, the sudden drop is breathtaking and the view is wide and far. The greensand hills to the north are dominated by the skyline town of Shaftesbury.

The Trust's holding extends for three miles eastwards into Cranborne Chase, up a long dry valley on the north side of Compton Abbas Airfield, and reaches the Ox Drove on the Wiltshire county boundary. These eastern parts comprise one of the finest areas of unspoilt chalk downland in Dorset and are rich floristically and in their butterflies, the adonis blue and fritillaries being particularly prolific. Small blocks of woodland include clumps of old holly and the delightfully named Cat's Whisker Plantation.

*Trust ownership:* 443 acres. Of this, the first 97 acres on Melbury Hill, including Melbury Beacon, was bought in 1986 through a Nature Conservancy Council grant and bequests from Miss D. Bushby, R.O. Leggett, and E.J. Taylor. The Nature Conservancy also helped finance the subsequent acquisitions, with contributions from the Countryside Commission and the Trust's Wessex Fund. 54 acres, north of Melbury Beacon, were added to the holding later in 1986. Then came 49 acres, east of Melbury Beacon, in 1987. Melbury Down, with its great dry valley of 243 acres, was acquired the same year.

*Location and access:* This holding extends from just north of Whitehall, on the valley road between Compton Abbas and Cann, to within 150 yards of the B3081 on Ashmore Down – nearly five miles to the east. It is currently served by a small car-park on Spread Eagle Hill, towards the centre of the holding, but the road system is set to change with proposals to by-pass Compton Abbas by moving the A350 out of the Blackmore Vale and into these uplands of Cranborne Chase.

**Melbury Down** – see entry for **Melbury Beacon**

**Melbury Hill** – see entry for **Melbury Beacon**

**Middlebere Peninsula**, Arne – see entry for **Hartland Moor National Nature Reserve**

**Monmouth** – for claimant to the throne and rebellion leader **James Scott, Duke of Monmouth** [1649-85] see entries for **Brownsea Island/ Seatown/** and **Ware Cliffs**

**Montgomery** – for **General (Sir) Bernard Montgomery** [later Field Marshal and first Viscount Montgomery of Alamein, 1887-1976] see entries for **Old Harry Rocks (Fort Henry)** and **Studland Heath National Nature Reserve (Project Fougasse)**

**Mountbatten** – for commando chief **Acting Admiral Louis Mountbatten** [later first Earl Mountbatten of Burma, 1900-79] see entry for **Studland Heath National Nature Reserve**

**Murillo** – for painter **Bartolomé Murillo** [1617-82] see entry for **Kingston Lacy House**

**Nature Reserves of English Nature** – see entries for **Hartland Moor National Nature Reserve/ Holt Heath National Nature Reserve/** and **Studland Heath National Nature Reserve**

**New Mills Heath**, Corfe Castle – see entry for **Hartland Moor National Nature Reserve**

**Nine Barrow Down**, Corfe Castle – see entry for **Ailwood Down**

**Norchard Farm**, Stanton St Gabriel – see entry for **Stanton St Gabriel**

**North Hill Plantation**, Chedington – see entry for **Winyard's Gap**

**Old Harry Rocks:** aerial view of what the maps call 'The Foreland or Handfast Point' with the Old Harry collection of chalk-stacks in the near distance and the Haystack and the Pinnacle behind. The next headland is Ballard Point with Swanage beyond. Photograph: Richard Riding.

**Obelisks** – see entries for **Godlingston Manor (Ballard Down Obelisk)** and **Kingston Lacy House (The Park)**

## OLD HARRY ROCKS, HANDFAST POINT, TURF RICK ROCK, THE PINNACLE, KING BARROW, STUDLAND CASTLE (lost), PARSON'S BARN, FORT HENRY, BALLARD CLIFF, and MANOR FARM

*between Studland and Swanage*                                    SZ 055 824

*Landforms – the chalk stacks (SZ 056 825):* Sea erosion at Old Harry Rocks is constantly cutting separate blocks of chalk, called 'stacks', which become detached from the parent cliff. The slender one at the end of The Foreland or Handfast Point, the eastern extremity of the Isle of Purbeck, is Old Harry and he had a plump wife until she drowned in the 1898 gale that destroyed the old chain pier at Brighton.

*The devil by any other name:* Old Harry was the Devil, and appropriately the main clifftop beside him is known as Old Nick's Ground. The detached cliff between the coastal path and Old Harry is called No Man's Land. The gap between it and the mainland is Saint Lucas Leap, reputedly taking its name from a pedigree greyhound that didn't quite make the jump when coursing a hare. Collectively these are Old Harry Rocks, though the headland is also known to the map-makers (though to no one else) as The Foreland or Handfast Point.

The two other detached rocks, to the south towards Ballard Point, are Turf Rick Rock [locally known as The Haystack] and The Pinnacle. Both are named for their shapes. The big sea-cave between them is Parson's Barn [*see its entry below*].

*King Barrow (SZ 046 820):* A Bronze Age round barrow, a burial mound of about 1,800 BC, that is forty-five feet in diameter and four feet high. It lies at the centre of the peninsula, between Studland village and Ballard Down, in an unploughed corner two hundred and fifty yards east of the Warren Wood. The mound has been opened at the centre, but the results went unrecorded.

Another barrow, since destroyed, was known as the Cracker Barrow and stood to the west of the Glebeland Estate at map reference *SZ 035 817*.

*Ancient fields (SZ 040 820):* Sixty-five acres of Ballard Down and Handfast Point were covered with the extensive remains of Iron Age and Romano-British Celtic field systems, with the probability that further areas, between the four main mapable blocks, had been

Old Harry Rocks, between Studland and Swanage: chalk-stacks with this view being from the main promontory towards the next, with the Haystack offshore and topped with cormorants, at the eastern end of the Purbeck Hills. Photograph: Colin Graham.

obliterated by mediaeval ploughing. Almost all traces above ground have now been flattened by late twentieth century ploughing.

The best preserved group was formerly a twelve-acre block of small enclosures, varying from square shapes to rectangles stretching up the slope, on the northern side of the down (*SZ 035 815*). Some of the lynchets were eight feet high. The contemporary access route was a banked trackway that approached from lower ground to the north-east and ran diagonally up through the enclosures until being blocked on the 400 feet contour by the two-feet high scarp-line of the southern-most field.

Tracks such as this indicate that the probable location of one of the adjacent ancient settlements of native farmers is covered by the Warren Wood (*SZ 043 821*).

*Studland Castle* (lost, at *SZ 056 826*): Until about 1770, Studland Castle jutted north-eastwards from the present Old Harry Rocks. It was a blockhouse, one of Henry VIII's series of coastal forts, built about 1540 for heavy guns to protect England from continental retaliation after the king had split from the Roman Catholic church.

It was built with low stone walls, with a slanting angle or 'batter', to withstand the new age of gunpowder. A second castle was constructed at the eastern end of Brownsea Island [*see its entry*] and together they guarded the approaches to the mouth of Poole Harbour.

Studland Castle was sited next to an earlier castle "upon which it abuteth". Both Studland castles have been claimed by the sea but there must be some stonework surviving in the rock pools.

*Parson's Barn smugglers' cave* (*SZ 053 823*): Accessible only by boat, the big sea-cave between Turf Rick Rock and The Pinnacle was used by smugglers in the eighteenth and nineteenth centuries.

It takes its name from its spaciousness because in the days of tithes there was nothing more accommodating than the Parson's Barn. Nor was there a category of person more appreciative of the fact that stolen waters were sweet.

*Fort Henry* (*SZ 038 828*): The great Fort Henry observation post is in the sycamore trees at the top of Redend Point at the southern end of Studland Beach. It is off the public path system though the National Trust is investigating the possibilities of public access to it.

The bunker was built by Canadian engineers in 1943 and can be glimpsed end-on if you look to the left of the pine trees that stand to

**Old Harry Rocks, Studland: from the next outcrop to the east, the rock-pools beneath Redend Point and Fort Henry wartime blockhouse. Photograph: Colin Graham.**

**Old Harry Rocks side of Studland Bay: Fort Henry, on Redend Point, was the Second World War VIP observation post from which Winston Churchill and King George VI watched the massive rehearsals for the invasion of Normandy. The recessed ridges of the eye-level slit protected them from air attack. Photograph: Colin Graham.**

your right as you descend the steps on to Studland beach from the Middle Beach car-park.

It is one of Britain's most important relics of the Second World War, being an immense concrete structure ninety feet long with an eye-level observation slit recessed into its almost three feet thick walls for a length of more than eighty feet.

Here, in the spring of 1944, stood King George VI, Prime Minister Winston Churchill, General Dwight D. Eisenhower (Supreme Commander Allied Expeditionary Force), General Sir Bernard Montgomery (effectively, for the assault, commander-in-chief Allied land forces, commanding the British 21st Army Group), General Omar Bradley (commanding the First United States Army), and Lieutenant-General Miles Dempsey (commanding the Second British Army).

They watched live explosions provide reality to Exercise Smash which assaulted the Studland sands in major rehearsals for the launching of the Second Front on the shores of Normandy.

The King's visit was especially loud, being arranged to coincide with a demonstration of aerial carpet or pattern bombing. The royal train, bringing Churchill and Montgomery as well, arrived in Swanage. Then police toured the town and eastern Purbeck to warn people to open all their windows – to minimise blast damage as the ground shook to the concussive thud of Studland's war.

There is a detailed account of this activity in my book on *Dorset at War: Diary of WW2* [1990].

[*See also the entry for Studland Heath National Nature Reserve*]

*Ballard Cliff wartime radar and gun-laying posts* (*SZ 044 813*): There is the site of a rifle range on the downland at the top of Ballard Cliff, the headland at the northern end of Swanage Bay, and concrete footings show the site of what seems to have been a Royal Air Force coastal radar station.

In 1940-41 there was also a Royal Artillery observation post at the seaward end of Ballard Down, for gun-laying which directed the fall of shot from two sixteen-inch railway mounted howitzers which were concealed in sidings on the heath at Furzebrook, to the north-west of Corfe Castle, as part of the anti-invasion defences.

*Ashes of H.G. Wells:* The ashes of Herbert George Wells [1866-1946], the radical author and futurist, were scattered from a boat into the sea off Old Harry Rocks.

It seemed appropriate as a passage from his work that was read at the memorial service had concluded: "We are all things that make and pass, striving upon a hidden mission, out to the open sea."

*Landscape:* The area of headland described in this entry is the eastern peninsula of the Purbeck chalklands. It projects into Poole Harbour and forms a backdrop of white cliffs to both Studland and Swanage bays.

The views are of Bournemouth and the Isle of Wight. Redend Point, at the south end of Studland's main beach, is an outcrop of gritty sandstone of the Bagshot beds and has visible layers of grey ball clay which causes sticky patches on the shoreline. There are many old prints and pictures of this spectacular stretch of coast in my *Guide to Purbeck Coast and Shipwreck* [1984].

From 1960 to 1990 there were few kinds things to be said for the great open slope extending from the very top of Ballard Down and sweeping across to the fringes of Studland village and the coast path. Firstly, there is the suburban implant of the 1930s chalets of the Glebeland Estate, set half a mile south of the village at the centre of the hillside, just about all of which have been extended out of all recognition into modern luxury homes. That it was ever built is said to have been because landowner Ralph Bankes's agent missed the train for the London auction at which the church authorities sold the land. Mature gardens now soften its impact.

The second abuse of the landscape was its conversion into a vast cereal acreage, though hardly a prairie as these flinty coastal slopes were never going to be highly productive grainlands, no matter how much fertilizer and subsidies were thrown at them.

The farming operation centres on Manor Farm, on the south side of Studland village, and when its tenancy fell-in for reletting in 1991 the National Trust removed 200 acres from the holding. These are being restored to natural grassland or woodland, most with public access, and the land retained for normal farming is being managed with traditional crop rotation and a return to dairying.

On the other side of Studland, between the western part of the village and the southern edge of Studland Heath, the Trust is also allowing a corridor of fields to revert to semi-natural pasture land as a quiet area for wildlife and the comparatively few non-coastal walkers.

*Trust ownership:* 1,100 acres, part of the Corfe Castle Estate, left to the Trust by Ralph Bankes on his death in 1981.

*Location and access:* The coastal footpath from Studland to Swanage follows the clifftop of the peninsula to Old Harry Rocks [one mile] and Ballard Cliff [two miles].

Park in Studland village at the Middle Beach car-park. Take the lane southwards beside the Manor House Hotel. It becomes a track. Take note that access to Studland often has to be fought for; an early start is essential on hot summer weekends or you'll find the police have closed the road from Corfe Castle because of overcrowding.

The alternative is to follow the access details given in the Ballard Down entry. Ballard Cliff immediately adjoins this holding and Old Harry Rocks are a mile further along the path, to the north.

Oswald – for the stone seat to **Major William Digby Oswald** [1880-1916] see entry for **The Hardy Monument**

**Owermoigne** parish – see entry for **South Down Farm, Sea Barn Farm, Ringstead Bay, Burning Cliff, and White Nothe**

**Paintings** – see entry for **Kingston Lacy House**

Palgrave – for adventure writer **Mary Palgrave** [nineteenth century] see entries for **Corfe Castle** and **Godlingston Manor**

## PAMPHILL ANTIQUITIES, MANOR HOUSE, GREEN and CRICKET PAVILION, KINGSTON LACY GARDENS, HILLBUTTS, ABBOTT STREET, and CHILBRIDGE
*north-west of Wimborne*                                    ST 990 006

*Pamphill Antiquities:* This is a Bronze Age round barrow, a burial mound, on the rise above the cottages at the eastern end of the village of Little Pamphill (*ST 995 002*). The woodlands at Pamphill preserve two sections of the causeway of the Roman road from Badbury Rings to Hamworthy, through Abbott Street Copse (*ST 985 007*) and Grove Wood (*ST 987 005*). There is also a later earthwork of unknown purpose in Abbott Street Copse (*ST 985 006*).

*Pamphill Manor House (ST 989 006):* Fine two-storey brick country house in William and Mary style, built at the end of the seventeenth century by Matthew Beethell, who was Sir Ralph Bankes's steward. It

Pamphill Antiquities, near Wimborne: relics abound and the landscape is itself historic, encapsulating mediaeval land-use with glimpses of the past clustered around an unspoilt village green. Photograph: Rodney Legg.

is leased as a private residence and does not have any public access, either to the house or grounds, but can be glimpsed from the avenue that crosses Pamphill Green, on the opposite side of Abbott Street from St Stephen's Church.

*Pamphill Green (ST 990 008)*: Matches the idyll of the village green, cricket included, as well as any in England. Surrounded by fine trees and thatched roofs. Unfenced lanes skirt through tongues of common land and no main road traffic spoils the tranquillity. The avenue of oaks was planted in 1846.

It is a registered village green (VG8, 12.14 hectares) with the area of registration including not only the main part, between the school and church drive, but also the south-eastern part. This is called Little Pamphill and faces a row of thatched cottages and the Trust-owned Vine public house. The cottages of Pamphill date from the eighteenth century and were built on common land by the exercise of one year's squatters' rights.

*Cricket pavilion (ST 989 007)*: The rustic thatched cricket pavilion was built in 1907 and is a delightful semi-modern contribution to this mediaeval dream-land.

*Church and almshouses (ST 988 009 and ST 993 004)*: Though not actually owned by the Trust, Pamphill's two public buildings are surrounded by its land and also fit perfectly into the scene. The Edwardian parish church, St Stephen's, built in 1906, could look suburban but is saved by the leafy canopies that are the backdrop to the north side of the green.

The range of almshouses and school buildings, combined under one roof in a more open setting at the south end of the green, would not look out of place anywhere. Like the manor they are neat William and Mary brickwork and a tablet records them as the "pious and charitable gift of Roger Gillingham", in 1698, "to God and ye poor".

The Trust supports the school and encourages its participation in conservation projects on the estate.

*Kingston Lacy Gardens (ST 979 007)*: The derelict corner of Pamphill, without any public access, comprised in 1985 the smashed greenhouses and overgrown vines and herb-beds of the kitchen garden for Kingston Lacy House. It had become a sad shambles but such was its reputation in its heyday that Queen Victoria sent her royal gardeners here for refresher courses. Most of the site has now been cleared.

*Hillbutts (ST 996 010)*, *Abbott Street (ST 991 009)* and *Chilbridge (ST 992 013)*: Dorset vernacular architecture at its best; scatterings of thatched cottages of varied shapes and building materials. Some have mud or chalk cob walls, on foundations of gritty heathstone, though mostly they have been subsequently clad in bricks.

*Landscape:* Very much Home Counties rather than West Country, with the best of the sort of architecture and rural cameos you can find in Surrey gathered together in a single package and without the traffic.

The scene used to be much more three dimensional, being dominated – particularly around Hound Hill, Hillbutts and Tadden – by the tallest elms in Dorset. They were in almost every hedgerow, as indeed are their table-top stumps, until the devastation of Dutch elm disease in the 1970s.

I enthused over them in 1969, shortly before the arrival of bark beetles carrying the lethal fungus: "In November the approach of winter ceased and autumn leaves lingered on the trees. Every leaf seemed to cling to the last and the elms were the most splendid with soft and delicate yellows replacing the green. Even when the turned leaves had passed their best they continued to stick.

"The great elms at Kingston Lacy were the finest of all, and beat any in the elmier landscape of the Blackmore Vale. In past years the beech looked best, but against these elms the Badbury Rings avenue was a harsh, unvarying brown."

*Trust ownership:* 1,400 acres, part of the lands left to the Trust by Ralph Bankes who died in 1981. The Vine public house was purchased in 1989.

*Location and access:* A mile north-west of Wimborne, off the B3082 [Blandford] road. Take the third turning off the south side of this road, at Hillbutts – the group of cottages to the west of Queen Elizabeth's School. You then come to Pamphill Green in a third of a mile. The church is to the right and the manor, cricket pavilion and almshouses are down the opposite lane, to the left.

Kingston Lacy Gardens do not have any public access but were visible from the road, Abbott Street, half a mile west of Pamphill Green and opposite Chalk Pit Coppice.

**Pamphill** parish – see entries for **Cowgrove Common, Mediaeval Moot, Court House, Lower Dairy Cottage, Walnut Farm, and**

Pilsdon Pen, near Broadwindsor: superlative scenery, in its own right and for the fact that the entrenchments of the summit plateau encompass the highest point in Dorset – at 908 feet above sea level. Photograph: Colin Graham.

**Eye Ford/ King Down and Beech Avenue** (listed under Badbury Rings)/ **Kingston Lacy House, including the Park, Philae Needle and other Egyptology/ Lodge Farm/** and **Pamphill Antiquities, Manor House, Green and Cricket Pavilion, Kingston Lacy Gardens, Hillbutts, Abbott Street and Chilbridge**

**The Park**, Pamphill – see entry for **Kingston Lacy House**

**Parson's Barn**, Studland – see entry for **Old Harry Rocks**

**Penney's Hill Coppice**, Chedington – see entry for **Winyard's Gap**

**Philae Needle**, Pamphill – see entry for **Kingston Lacy House**

**Pilsdon** parish – see entry for **Pilsdon Pen**

## PILSDON PEN
*west of Broadwindsor*                                    *ST 414 012*

*Hill-fort:* Major Iron Age hill-fort with triple banks and ditches between, built by iron-using Celtic settlers from across the Channel after 200 BC. They enclosed nine acres of a flat-topped spur. Their key weapon was the sling, firing rounded pebbles.

This important Durotrigic fortress probably superseded the Trust-owned string of smaller forts [Lambert's Castle, Coney's Castle, Lewesdon Hill] that can be seen from its ramparts. Excavation has revealed areas of stained soil that mark the sites of wattle and daub huts and a spread of coarse, blackened pottery. Gold-smelting crucibles were the outstanding finds, together with a Romano-Celtic temple. It was a large building, about fifty yards square, and slingstones were found along its foundations.

The dig, which took place from 1963 to 1971, also uncovered evidence that Pilsdon Pen may have been one of the native fortress stormed by Vespasian's Second Legion, probably towards the end of its conquest of the West, about AD 45-46. They found a Roman spearhead and ballista bolt. The latter indicates that a heavy artillery piece was hauled up the hill – which would hardly have been done for other than an attack.

*Name:* Pilsdon is the name of the parish [though it is quite likely that it takes its name from the hill] and 'Pen' is an old English word for an enclosure that held stock.

*Landscape:* Pilsdon Pen is a great chert plateau, with the distinction at 908 feet of being the highest point in Dorset. It has a distant view to Dartmoor and a near one of the Marshwood Vale – spread out below and fringed by Trust-owned hills – and the coastline of Lyme Bay. The seaward extremities are Portland Bill in the east and Start Point to the south-west. On the exposed hilltop the impoverished soil favours a tough flora which includes gorse and bilberries.

*Trust ownership:* 36 acres, bought from the Pinney family in 1979 with money bequeathed by Miss P.A. Hardcastle and Miss E.V.A. Compton in memory of Leslie Spencer Compton.

*Location and access:* Dominates the B3164 between Broadwindsor and Birdsmoor gate, where the B3164 joins the B3165 road (Lyme Regis to Crewkerne). Parking is at the foot of the hill in a layby beside the turning to Pilsdon. Cross the road to the stile. It is a stiff climb to the top.

**The Pinnacle**, Studland – see entry for **Old Harry Rocks**

Piombo – for Italian painter **Sebastiano del Piombo** [1485-1547] see entry for **Kingston Lacy House**

Pissarro – landscape painter **Lucien Pissarro** [1863-1944] produced a number of works in the vicinity of **Fishpond Bottom, Whit[e]church Canonicorum** which feature what is now National Trust scenery. See the entry for **Lambert's Castle Hill**.

Popham – for semaphore surveyor **Rear-Admiral Sir Home Riggs Popham** [1762-1820] see entry for **Lambert's Castle Hill**.

**Portesham** parish – see entry for the **Hardy Monument**

**PORTLAND HOUSE**
*at Weymouth*                                               *ST 680 779*

*Portland House:* Split-level Spanish hacienda-style art-deco villa, designed for the Bushby family in 1935 by architect Gerald Wellesley, later the seventh Duke of Wellington [1885-1972]. There is a magnificent staircase descending from the upper to lower ground-floors with curved and bevelled treads and tiled risers. The Crittal-Hope windows are the forerunner of galvanised metal casements. Exterior paintwork is "Delphinium Blue," the Trust's management plan continues. "The original colours have always been retained when decorating the house both inside and out and R.G. Spiller and Sons, Fleet Street, Beaminster, have always done the decorating." The stables, lodge and garage belonged to an earlier house. The property is the gem of the clifftop Belle Vue conservation area.

*War damage:* Portland House suffered roof damage from German bombs on several occasions during the Second World War and more extensive repairs were necessary after Junkers Ju88 bombers attacked Bincleaves Groyne on 5 June 1941. Offshore they sank the *Himalaya* coal-hulk. A hundred yards east of the house was a 40mm Bofors anti-aircraft gun, firing 120 rounds a minute.

*Landscape:* Superb formal gardens, with sweeping lawns and a colonnade of palms to enhance the Spanish atmosphere, overlooking Portland Harbour and its massive breakwaters. Bincleaves Groyne begins 250 yards to the north-east. This was built between 1894-1903 and completed the Royal Navy's "Harbour of Refuge". Two hundred yards along it, projecting towards Portland House, are the buildings and jetty of the Bincleaves Torpedo Range which in recent years has been used by the Special Boat Service of the Royal Marines. There is also considerable helicopter activity, from HMS Osprey air-base on the other side of the largest man-made harbour in the world. It encloses four square miles of deep water. Immediately offshore are the Western Ledges.

*Trust ownership:* 6 acres, of which 4.53 acres are the grounds with 0.732 acres of foreshore and cliffs, given by Miss Dorothy Esther Bushby in 1970 and passing to the Trust in 1985.

*Location and access:* On the south side of Bell Vue Road at Rodwell, Weymouth. The house is not open to the public though it is hoped that in the future the gardens may be open at appropriate times of the year under the National Gardens Scheme. The only permanent public access is the coastal footpath, from Newton's Cove to Sandsfoot Castle, which crosses the property. This section of Weymouth public footpath number 125 is known as Underbarn Walk.

Powys – for Dorset essayist **Llewelyn Powys** [1884-1939] see the entry for **South Down Farm (White Nothe, or Nose as he called it)**

Pratt – for architect **Sir Robert Pratt** [1620-84] see entry for **Kingston Lacy House**

**Priest's Way**, Langton Matravers – see entry for **Seacombe Bottom**

**Puckstone**, Studland – see entry for **Studland Heath National Nature Reserve**

**Puncknowle** parish – see entry for **West Bexington, Limekiln Hill, Tulk's Hill, Labour-in-Vain Farm, and the Chesil Beach**

**Punfield Cove**, Swanage – see entry for **Whitecliff Farm**

**Purbeck amenity woodland** – see entry for **Wilkswood Farm**. For the **Island of Purbeck** generally, see parish listings for **Arne, Corfe Castle, Langton Matravers, Steeple, Studland, Swanage, and Worth Matravers**

**Redhorn Quay**, Studland – see entry for **Studland Heath National Nature Reserve**

Redvers – for Norman rebel baron **Baldwin de Redvers** [died 1155] see entries for **Corfe Castle** and **Corfe Common (The Rings)**

Richmond – for archaeologist (Sir) **Ian Richmond** [1902-65] see entry for **Hod Hill**

**Ridge Cliff**, Chideock – see entry for **Seatown**

**RINGMOOR and TURNWORTH DOWN**
*above Okeford Fitzpaine*                              *ST 816 084*
*Romano-British settlement (ST 080 085)*: Ringmoor is a major complex of ancient earthworks that are remarkably well preserved. They are grouped around and oval bank twelve feet across and four feet high,

which would have been stockaded to protect the settlement and has a ditch on the outside. It lies in the centre of the eastern part of the open downland field at 750 feet above sea level. There are traces of levelled spaces, for buildings.

To the south, west and north-east run three trackways which led to the fields. These were in the angles between the tracks and all the ground that is at present clear of vegetation has traces of the low banks of Celtic field systems. These fields were small by modern standards, being between half an acre and three acres.

*Landscape:* Ringmoor is an oasis of open downland in an area that is otherwise under the plough or canopied by ancient or modern woodland. The Trust's land also includes some fine old deciduous woods of ash and oak under-stood with coppiced hazel. From the open areas there are views across the chalklands of central Dorset.

*Trust ownership:* 134 acres, bought in 1978 with bequests from J.F. Kingzett, Miss A.W. St Paul, W.G. Duncombe, a donation from the Fontmell Fund, and a Countryside Commission grant.

*Location and access:* Five miles north of the A354. Turn off at Winterborne Whitechurch, along the valley road through Winterborne Stickland and Turnworth, towards Okeford Fitzpaine.

Half a mile after Turnworth village you park on the west side of this lane. There is open access to the whole property. To find Ringmoor you follow Turnworth bridleway number 7, just inside the southern perimeter of the Trust land, for nearly half a mile. Ringmoor is the triangular-shaped western extremity of the holding. The prehistoric Ridgeway runs along the edge of the nearby escarpment.

**The Rings,** Corfe Castle – see entry for **Corfe Common**

**Ringstead Bay** – see entry for **South Down Farm**

Roebuck – for signals engineer **George Roebuck** [early nineteenth century] see entry for **Lambert's Castle Hill**

**Roman remains** – see entries for **Badbury Rings (Vindocladia and Crab Farm Roman Fort)/ Brownsea Island (Pottery)/ Cerne Giant (Hill-figure)/ Hod Hill (Roman Conquest and fort)/ Melbury**

Beacon (Romano-British ranch boundary)/ Pamphill Antiquities (Roman road and earthworks) / Pilsdon Pen (Roman Conquest and temple)/ Ringmoor (Romano-British settlement)/ and Wilkswood Farm (Roman Marble Industry also with entry for Woodhouse Hill Roman Buildings, Studland)

Romano – for Italian painter **Giulio Pippe de'Gianuzzi**, known as **Giulio Romano** [1499-1546] see entry for **Kingston Lacy House**

**Round barrows** – see entries for **Ailwood Down (Nine Barrow Down)/ Badbury area finds/ Badbury Rings (Straw Barrow Group, King Down Barrows, Barrows south-west of Badbury Rings)/ Corfe Common (Barrow Group)/ Godlingston Manor (Barrows listed)/ Golden Cap (Cairns)/ Hardown Hill (Barrows)/ Holt Heath National Nature Reserve (Bull Barrow)/ Kingswood Barrows and Fishing Barrow Group/ Melbury Beacon (Barrows)/ Old Harry Rocks (Kings Barrow)/ Pamphill Antiquities (Little Pamphill green)/ Thorncombe Beacon (Barrows)/ West Bexington (Tulk's Hill)/ and Whitecliff Farm (Ballard Down)**

Rubens – for Flemish painter **Peter Paul Rubens** [1577-1640] see entry for **Kingston Lacy House**

Russell – for mathematician and philosopher **Bertrand Russell** [later third Earl Russell, 1872-1970] see entry for **Studland Village (Cliff End)**

**St Gabriel's Church** – see entry for **Stanton St Gabriel**

**SAINT WITE'S WELL and SHIP FARM**
*south of Morcombelake*                                                      *SY 400 940*
*Saint Wite's Well (SY 399 937)*: Lying by the track at the foot of the eastern slope of Chardown Hill, this sacred well is a mile from the martyr's shrine, which is in Whit[e]church Canonicorum parish church.
It is known as "Saint Vita's Well" to the people of Morcombelake and

Saint Wite's Well, near Morcombelake: shrine to a martyr of the Dark Ages, its waters are reputed to cure failing sight. It has been provided with a modern kerb. Photograph: Colin Graham.

was an "eye-well" that provided "a sovereign cure for sore eyes" if the dousing took place in the first light of a new day; perhaps the time of day contributed to the general shock. Bent pins were dropped in the well-head with the request: "Holy well, holy well, take my gift and cast a spell."

Thomas Gerard, writing in the 1620s, says Saint Wite "lived in prayer and contemplation" near Whit[e]church, "not far off in the side of a hill", which perfectly describes this spot. Local people are quite certain, and for years the well-site has been shown by the Ordnance Survey in the gothic type that depicts antiquity. "The Saint's Well" is says on the current 6-inch map.

In the mid-1980s, before restoring a stone kerb to the site of the well, the National Trust would not admit that the spring was a holy well. "There is no absolute proof," they said, and passed on the verdict of the county archaeologist that it is merely an ancient spring. Nevertheless, warden Toby Eaton was prepared to compromise by calling it the "Saint's Well' – which is where the Ordnance Survey arrived many years ago, and which begs an inevitable question. Which saint?

Local people had no doubt and knew the periwinkles on Stonebarrow Hill as "Saint Candida's Eyes". Candida is a latinisation of Saint Wite's name and the plant-name also perpetuates the connection with eye-cures. Christine Waters is also without any doubts and her booklet entitled *Who Was Saint Wite?* [sold in Whit[e]church Canonicorum church] calls it Saint Wite's Well and says that the side of the field around the well-head was allowed to become smothered in brushwood in the 1930s, to prevent cattle stumbling in, and the spring piped into a trough. The old kerbing disappeared and the modern trough is a replacement.

*About Saint Wite:* The Norman latinisation to Candida was on the wrongful assumption that "Wite" meant "White". Wite is thought to have been with the team of fifty who went with Saint Boniface of Crediton on his final mission to Germany. It ended with a massacre at Dockum, near Utrecht, on 5 June 755.

Boniface's remains were carried to the abbey at Fulda but it is unlikely that those of his minions could have been brought back to Britain for burial. Few of our war dead were returned in the twentieth century and the freight problems of the Dark Ages must have been inordinately prohibitive.

Anyway, Archbishop Cuthbert of Canterbury decreed to a shocked emergency synod that "Saint Boniface and his cohort should have their martyrdoms celebrated annually throughout the Church in England at Whitsuntide." This quote has since been distorted to read the "Church of England" – what he meant was the Church of Rome in England.

That was the time for the yearly dedicatory festival of at Whit[e]church Canonicorum, until it was changed in the reign of Henry VIII, though Whitsun must have seemed as good a time as any to celebrate Saint "White".

Local tradition does not go along with the Boniface connection and insists that Wite was killed by Danish pirates in a raid on Charmouth in the ninth century. Historians have stated this raid to be an absolute fact but the present author has uncovered no contemporary evidence.

The only certainty in all this is that Wite's thirteenth century tomb at Whit[e]church Canonicorum is one of only two martyrs' shrines that have survived intact in the whole of England. Its top is a stone chest of Purbeck marble, with three egg-shaped openings below, into which even today are placed pathetic offerings of money and cards and notes begging her intercession on behalf of the sick. The chest was damaged by subsidence in the winter of 1899 and in April 1900 repairs were carried out. Inside, on its edge at the north side, there was an oblong lead reliquary, twenty-nine inches long, inscribed "+HIC.REQUESCT.RELIQUE.SCE.WITE" [Here rest the relics of Saint Wite]. There were signs that it may have been opened in the sixteenth century. At the top was a thigh-bone, fourteen inches in length, and the bones were described as "the remains of a small woman, apparently about forty years old".

About 1910 some relics were found in Lambeth Palace that included one labelled "the thigh-bone of Saint Candida" (her Latin name) which validated an old local tradition that one of the thigh-bones was missing from the tomb. It was the custom, when an archbishop translated a saint's bones, for him to take one with him.

*Landscape:* The well is set in the small fields of a hillside dairy farm a short distance from the busy coast road at Morcombelake.

*Trust ownership:* 39 acres, bought in 1969 with money left to the Trust by R.I. Gunn.

*Location and access:* Ship Farm lies off the A35 between Lyme Regis and Bridport, at the west end of Morcombelake. It is on the seaward side of the road. There is a lane past the farm that climbs Chardown Hill

**Scotland Farm, near Corfe Castle:** the back wall, built in 1665 from the rubble of the ruined mediaeval castle, plus a pastoral touch. Photograph: Colin Graham.

to the Trust's parking and picnic area on the top. This green lane has no vehicular right of way and is only a bridleway. Cars are prohibited, so to reach the Stonebarrow Hill car-park you have to approach from the other side, up Stonebarrow Lane from just east of the river bridge at Charmouth [the old course of the A35 now the by-pass is completed]. Park at the far end of the car-park by the pine trees. Take the green lane marked "Morcombelake".

Walk downhill for half a mile to the track on the right just before you reach Ship Farm. The well is about two hundred yards along this byway [midway to the bungalow known as Coldharbour] in the field to the right.

**Saxon cross-base**, Studland – see entry for **Studland Village**

## SCOTLAND FARM and SHARFORD BRIDGE
*north of Corfe Castle*                                    *SY 961 841*

*Sharford Bridge (SY 967 848)*: Packhorse bridge over the Corfe River, reached by public paths, three of them bridleways, from four directions. One of the bridleways comes from the east, from Trust-owned South Middlebere. The Trust's lands touch the little publicly-maintained bridge at its north-west corner.

From the south-west there is a second bridleway, from the Trust's Scotland Farm, but the final field in this direction belongs to the Rempstone estate. Ditto everything on the other side of the river, where a bridleway goes to the south-east, up into the pine plantation of Bushey.

The fourth of these ancient routes, now a footpath, is northwards down the east bank of the river to Wytch Farm oilfield and Poole Harbour.

Sharford Bridge is stone-built with two arches and probably dates from the sixteenth century. It is shown as "Sherford Bridge" on John Speed's county map of 1610.

The parapets of the bridge were rebuilt by Dorset County Council after I created a fuss about it ruinous condition in 1971.

*Scotland Farm (SY 962 840)*: A low-ceiling stone-roofed farmhouse with attic rooms on the edge of New Mills Heath, midway between the Purbeck Hills and the backwaters of Poole Harbour. The walls are particularly fine, but secondhand – being blocks of ashlar from the ruins

**Scotland Farm, near Corfe Castle: master mason Derek Cartridge, looking down from the restored barn, carved by Corfe sculptor Jonathan Sells in 1990. Photograph: Rodney Legg.**

of Corfe Castle.

That bit of recycling took place in 1665, nineteen years after the fortress was demolished for losing the Civil War. The seventeenth century credentials and builder's initials, W.W. for William Whefer, are cut in stone above the porch doorway.

It is an attractive porch, in proportion with the low-slung lines of the building. There are chimney stacks at each end and some fine stone mullioned windows. The barn and geese complete an olde worlde farmyard setting which has the distinction of having been painted by Gordon Beningfield.

*Scotland Farm Barn:* Immediately north-west of the farmhouse, this is stone walled with a thatched roof. Its renovation by the National Trust is marked by a commemorative stone, dated 1990 and with the Trust's oak-sprig logo.

Less obvious, around the corner on the south-facing side of the building, is a larger than life head, carved in relief, which has been set in the wall. It is a brilliant piece of work, not only artistically but in terms of the idea and place – positioned just below the eaves – as a striking revival of Dorset's ancient Celtic traditions.

The features are those of master mason Derek Cartridge, who led the restoration team, carved by Jonathan Sells of Corfe Castle.

*New Mills Sluices (SY 968 842):* The early eighteenth century New Mills stood at the eastern extremity of the Trust's lands, on the Corfe River. Nothing survives of their extensive buildings or operations apart from elegant sluices with stone cutwaters which now carry Corfe Castle public footpath number 80 across the river.

Dated 1711, by a stone, the cutwaters also carry carved initials. The west cutwater proclaims the ownership of "WO" and the eastern one is inscribed for "NB". This moulded stonework is on the south side, facing upstream.

*Calcraft boundary stone (SY 963 842):* An older boundary stone with a rounded top is set in the hawthorn hedge next to a "BP Pipeline" marker beside Corfe Castle bridleway number 3.

The stone is cut on its east-facing side with the letters "C C C" for "Corfe Castle Calcraft" and shows the north-west corner of a enclave of the Calcraft family's Rempstone estate which stretched 400 yards into what was otherwise Bankes-owned land on this side of the Corfe River.

Seacombe Bottom, near Worth Matravers: shelving ledges of Purbeck stone, worked in cliff-edge quarry galleries with the stone being lowered on to boats. This view is from the Winspit side, close to the scene of the 'Halsewell' shipwreck. Photograph: Colin Graham.

The Calcraft family bought the Rempstone estate in 1757 and stayed until the end of the nineteenth century.

*Landscape:* Pastoral Purbeck in the valley of the Corfe River, with the Trust's lands at Scotland Farm preserving a network of little fields that were carved out of the heath. They show a tendency to revert to gorse.

Many are herb-rich meadows and the benign regime on the Trust's side of the river contrasts with the richer greens on the other side where many of the old hedges have been grubbed out and the land improved with fertilizers.

*Trust ownership:* 100 acres, part of the Corfe Castle Estate left to the Trust by Ralph Bankes who died in 1981.

*Location and access:* Turn east off the A351 at the "Wytch Farm Oilfield" roundabout, which lies 1.4 miles south of the Halfway Inn between Wareham and Corfe Castle. Then, in only 50 yards, you turn left along the lane signposted "Slepe 1 ½, Arne 3".

In just under a mile there is a ninety-degree left-hand bend with a thatched barn visible straight ahead, eighty yards up a track. This is Scotland. There is enough grass for one or two cars, by the stile and on the other side of the farm access road.

A public footpath goes up this road and passes between the barn and Scotland Farm before continuing into the fields and reaching the Corfe River at the New Mills sluices.

Another footpath strikes off south, across the stile, to Corfe Castle. A third public path, a bridleway, goes through the gate a hundred yards north of the corner. This track passes the Calcraft boundary stone and drops down to the Corfe River at Sharford Bridge.

**Sea Barn Farm** – see entry for **South Down Farm**

## SEACOMBE BOTTOM, HEDBURY, ACTON QUARRIES, EASTINGTON FARM, and the PRIEST'S WAY

*south-east of Worth Matravers*                                    *SY 984 767*

*Priest's Way (SY 979 778 to SY 997 779):* The Trust's mile of this ancient highway between Worth Matravers and Swanage is a wide droveway between stone walls. Its name dates back to the early Middle Ages when Swanage [or Sandwich] was a chapelry of Worth parish church and the priest had to trek between the two. As a road, however, it goes back to prehistoric times.

*Seacombe Quarries* (*SY 984 766*): These were the most fulsome veins of workable stone on the Purbeck coast and they have been fully exploited, leaving gaping galleries sliced into the western cliff at Seacombe Bottom and running under the hill and along the valley side. Here the stone is 'Portland' rather than Purbeck, taken out in blocks of fifteen tons, and the roofs in the quarries are up to twelve feet high. They are supported by a few huge pillars but inevitably there are rockfalls. Their makers never intended the galleries to stand for centuries and it is unsafe to wander about underground; even with a hard-hat as that would only give cosmetic protection.

These great quarries were in use from about 1700 to 1930 and there were Second World War clearances of spoil for runway hardcore to build the series of military aerodromes across the heathlands of the New Forest.

*The 'Halsewell' disaster* (*SY 983 765*): The *Halsewell* East Indiaman, outward bound from London for Bengal, was wrecked off Seacombe in a blizzard on 6 January 1786. The 758-ton ship was dashed to pieces, though intrepid quarrymen were later able to salvage cupboards, an hour-glass and other fittings. Captain Richard Pierce drowned with his two daughters and two nieces, five other young ladies, and most of the officers and crew. A total of 168 lives were lost.

There was, however, a daring rescue. Eighty-two men were hauled to safety up the cliffs by the quarrymen. The seamen had struggled on to a slanting stone since known as the Halsewell Rock [at the west edge of the Trust's lands, a short distance towards Winspit] and were pulled on to a ledge halfway up the cliff. This shelf was later called the Halsewell Quarry.

The site of the disaster is below the Halsewell Stile at the limits of the Trust's property along the coastal path, at the top of the precipitous cliff that continues westwards to Winspit.

It must be emphasised that not only is there no access to the quarry or the rock, either from the cliff or the shore, but it is exceedingly dangerous even to attempt a closer look.

*Seacombe's 'Halsewell' graves* (*SY 985 767*): The site of these, on the other hand, is accessible; though the cannon that marked them have disappeared. Oliver W. Farrer wrote in the *Purbeck Papers* in 1858:

"One other sad memorial remains; on the little path of flat grass

Seacombe Bottom, quarry galleries: cavernous openings, the length of the west side of the valley, nine feet high and extending deep into the hillside. This is literally undermined and in varying stages of collapse. Photograph: Colin Graham.

Seacombe Bottom, half a mile east of: Hedbury Quarry, a cliffside shelf worked in Victorian times, with a Napoleonic period cannon mounted on a display plinth and pointing seawards. Photograph: Colin Graham.

where the cliffs divide, and the stream, when there is a stream, falls over the cliff, may yet be seen the traces of four long graves. The spot is appropriate. As you stand by the almost obliterated mounds, the eye wanders over little but sea and sky, and the wild solitude of the spot accords with the sadness of the tragedy here played out."

Digging took place in 1972, in an attempt to uncover the graves, but it is hoped that the National Trust will forbid any further pseudo-intellectual curiosity. The dead have a right to some peace.

*Hedbury Quarry cannon (SY 993 767)*: The name derives from the Eidbury family who began the quarry in the eighteenth century. Annoyingly, the Ordnance Survey refuses to name it – even on the large-scale maps – but it is a large and conspicuous hole shelved out of the cliffs. Hedbury Quarry lies about half a mile east from Seacombe in the direction of Dancing Ledge and the coastal footpath detours around the top of it.

In 1960 I clambered around the quarry floor and found a twelve-pounder cannon of the Napoleonic period wedged between large blocks of semi-cut stone. The cannon was hauled out and re-set on a stone plinth, pointing seawards, in the mid 1970s. There is some ironwork on the cliff edge that shows the site of the 'whim', as the quarrymen called the crane that was used to lower cut stone into the boats that took it to Swanage. There was no roadway out of the quarry.

*Seacombe's gun-nest (ST 986 768)*: On the side of the eastern slopes overlooking Seacombe Bottom is a rounded metal turret which is often mistaken for the cockpit of a crashed aircraft. It was in fact put there in 1940, for a single machine-gunner who had the unenviable task of keeping watch on Seacombe in the months when invasion was a real threat. The gun would have been fired from the shuttered front which was the only opening into the canopy – the gunner had no back door from the war.

*Acton Quarries (SY 990 783)*: The Trust owns a series of open-cast stone quarries around the hamlet of Acton to the west of Langton Matravers. Some date back to the eighteenth century. Though the bulk of the modern output has been for aggregates, for road-making, rather than building stone, the Trust's own crop of character cottages generates a continuing demand for roofing slates and the better class

Seacombe Bottom entry: the Trust also owns the present-day quarries around the hamlet of Acton, where this is a typical stone-roofed Purbeck cottage, on the plateau beside the Priest's Way, above Langton Matravers. Photograph: Rodney Legg.

of restorations. Generally, the currently more restrained architectural climate is reviving the use of shaped blocks of cut stone.

The Trust intends to restore much of the worked-out land to agriculture but some disused quarries are being preserved for their industrial, archaeological and conservation interest. Abandoned underground workings provide nationally important bat roosts that are leased to the Dorset Trust for Nature Conservation.

*Landscape:* There is still downland turf on these central stone cliffs of southern Purbeck and the slopes of its limestone plateau. On top there are arable fields north of Eastington Farm and Sea Spray but the rough pastures extend inland up the coombes. The Trust's holding stretches to Abbascombe and Eastington Farm, and to the present-day quarrylands west of Acton.

*Trust ownership:* 850 acres, part of the Corfe Castle Estate bequeathed to the Trust by Ralph Bankes in 1981.

*Location and access:* Crossed by the coastal footpath from St Alban's Head to Durlston Head, but the most direct paths are from Worth Matravers [turn eastwards from just below the pond and cross the first ridge of hills into the next valley, then turn right, down the valley to Seacombe] which is a mile away.

Alternatively you can approach from the Swanage side. Park near Langton Matravers School and take the path via Dancing Ledge to the coastal footpath. Turn right, westwards, along the coastal path. You come first to Hedbury and then descend to Seacombe. Hedbury is a mile and a half away from Langton Matravers and Seacombe two miles.

## SEATOWN, RIDGE CLIFF, and WEST CLIFF
*seaward of Chideock*                                        *SY 422 920*

*First landing of Monmouth's rebels:* This took place on the shingle beach at Seatown (*SY 429 917*) on the morning of 11 June 1685 when two men rowed ashore. An English gentleman, Thomas Dare, was accompanied by Andrew, Lord Fletcher; a fiery Scot.

The latter was second-in-command of the Duke's cavalry and they slipped into Dorset as the advance party to organise the imminent attempt at seizing the throne for Monmouth, from his uncle, James II.

Their exploits charted a course for failure that would be consistent with that for the expedition as a whole. Fletcher pulled rank to commandeer Dare's horse. The Englishman refused and raised his whip; at which Fletcher shot him through the head.

Volunteers who witnessed the incident wanted Fletcher strung up for murder but he was smuggled back aboard ship and escaped to Spain. Nevertheless these were two disastrous own-goals for Monmouth's side. Fletcher could have been invaluable – an aggressive Scot was just what Monmouth lacked at the head of his cavalry for the skirmish at Bridport and the rout at the Battle of Sedgemoor. And Thomas Dare also had a vital position, as the paymaster for the operation.

*Packhorse bridge:* Over the River Winniford, 150 yards upstream from the Anchor Inn (*SY 422 918*), this carries Chideock public footpath number 13. It is an attractive yellow-stone humped bridge, dating from the eighteenth century, which was restored by the Manpower Services Commission in 1984, being cobbled with beach pebbles and given a new parapet.

*Smugglers:* As much as any in Dorset, because of homes near the beach and the absence of any nearby town or Coast Guard presence, the fishermen of Seatown had a reputation for being the most successful smugglers along this coast.

It was their achievement that brandy was kept below four shillings a bottle in Yeovil for almost the whole of the eighteenth century.

Rev C.V. Goddard, the vicar of Chideock in the 1890s, recorded smuggling tales from Seatown. Rev T. Worthington, a curate at Chideock in 1880, also wrote of the scale of the local free-trading: "Within the memory of some of the inhabitants there used to be from thirty to forty fishermen at Seatown, ostensibly employed in their lawful avocations, but really in smuggling.

"Not the fishermen only, but as in other seaside places half a century ago, the inhabitants in general were implicated in this contraband traffic, of which the sin, in their eyes, consisted only in being found out. Numerous stories are told of hair-breadth escapes from the clutches of the excise officers."

*Landscape:* Undercliff and cliff-sides rise from the little anchorage of Seatown where the River Winniford trickles through a high pebble bank into Lyme Bay.

These cliffs are of crumbling and slipping blue lias clay and the beach is stony. Dominating everything is the massive Golden Cap clifftop [*which has its own entry*]; 618 feet higher than the beach and a mile

**Seatown and Ridge Cliff: looking east, from the foothills of Golden Cap, with Portland jutting out along the horizon. Photograph: Colin Graham.**

Seatown, near Chideock: 'N.T. Packhorse Bridge restored by M.S.C. 1984' with cobbles from the pebble beach. It crosses the River Winniford. Photograph: Rodney Legg.

away. West Cliff is unstable and landslipped. Ridge Cliff, on the east side of Seatown, is a tilted pasture rising to 350 feet. It drops sheer into the sea at East Ebb and the Magging Stone.

*Trust ownership:* 170 acres, the greater part bought in 1966 through an anonymous donation to Enterprise Neptune. The remaining 25 acres were added from general Neptune funds in 1974.

*Location and access:* Off the A35 between Bridport and Lyme Regis. Turn south at Chideock. Sea Hill Lane, opposite the church, terminates in a non-Trust pay car-park beside the sea at Seatown. On each side the coastal footpath leads upwards into the Trust's lands.

Sebastiano - for Italian painter **Sebastiano del Piombo** [1485-1547] see entry for **Kingston Lacy House**

**Second World War** - see entries for **Brownsea Island (Clearing station for Aliens, 1940 fortifications, Major Strategic Night Decoy)/ Kingston Lacy House (Halifax bomber crash)/ Max Gate (RAF Warmwell commander's home)/ Old Harry Rocks (Fort Henry, VIP observation post)/ Stonebarrow Hill (Cain's Folly radar station)/ Studland Heath National Nature Reserve (Fougasse anti-invasion tests, Mountbatten's commandos, Exercise Smash, Studland Assault Training Beach)/ Studland Village (Heinkel bomber crash)/ Thorncombe Beacon (Pillbox, site of)/ West Bexington (Pillboxes)/ Whitecliff Farm (Ballard Down, radar apparatus)/** and **Winyard's Gap (43rd [Wessex] Division memorial)**

**Shapwick** parish - see entries for **Badbury Rings, Vindocladia, Crab Farm Roman Fort, Straw Barrow, and the Beech Avenue/** and **Shapwick Village, Market Cross, White Mill, and White Mill Bridge**

## SHAPWICK VILLAGE, MARKET CROSS, WHITE MILL, and WHITE MILL BRIDGE
*west of Wimborne*                                              *ST 937 017*

*Shapwick village:* Clustered around the church of St Bartholomew, which has a twelfth century north wall to its nave, are a number of seventeenth century and eighteenth century cottages. A settlement sprang up here in Roman times because it was the point where the important road from London, via Badbury Rings, to Dorchester crossed the River Stour. The river would then have been navigable at least up to here.

The cottages, most of which are Trust-owned and let to farmers and their hands, include several of mud-wall cob construction. In most cases, when they were a century old, they were given a brick cladding to extend their life. Any datestones, such as one from 1727, were added during such refurbishments. Some of the cottages are timber-framed and here and there you will spot original moulded timber windows. Inside most have chamfered beams and inglenook fireplaces with bread ovens though some of these features are concealed behind modern fireplaces.

The Trust owns the 'living', the ecclesiastical benefice, of St Bartholomew's Church. This is principally of interest for its fourteenth century tower and rebuilt nave which has several brasses dating from the following two hundred years. One is to Richard Chernock, 1538, and has the figure of a priest. A slate carries a charming epitaph of the sort that one often sees quoted but usually fails to find on site: "Anne Butler here beneath is laid/ a pious, prudent, modest maid." It is dated 1659 and set into the chancel floor.

*Market cross (ST 938 017)*: Beside the crossroads to the east of the church is an octagonal platform of brown heathstone with three steps and a base stone. These parts are fifteenth century but the cross itself is a memorial to twentieth century war dead.

*Bishop's Farm (ST 936 019)*: The middle section of Bishop's Farm, on the east bank of the Stour at the north end of the village, is the surviving part of Bishop's Court. John Hutchins's county history describes it as a "large capital dwelling house" and it is shown as Champagne Close on old maps. This preserves a memory of the gift of land by William the Conqueror to one of his Frenchmen, Peter de Champagne. The property later passed to De la lind Hussey and was bought by Colonel William Wake on his marriage to Ami Cutler.

They were to have a famous son, William Wake, in 1657. He was sent to Thomas Curganven's grammar school at Blandford and from there to Christ Church, Oxford, where he graduated BA, MA, BD and DD. Ordination followed and a chaplaincy in Paris. Back in England he became chaplain in ordinary to the new king and queen, William and Mary, in 1689. His career from scholar to prelate was now in motion and by 1705 he was Bishop of Lincoln.

He reached the pinnacle of the profession in 1716 by succeeding Thomas Tenison at Canterbury. Wake nearly organised a merger with disaffected French ecclesiastics and published numerous tracts on the *State of the Church* and the *Principles of the Christian Religion.* On four of his return visits to Shapwick he baptised his grandchildren in St Bartholomew's Church. Archbishop Wake died in 1737 at Lambeth Palace and is buried in Croydon. The Archbishop Wake First School perpetuates his name at Blandford.

Bishop's Court was bought by Henry Bankes in 1773 and rejoined the Kingston Lacy estate. It was soon largely rebuilt and had the Bankes arms set above the wide door arch.

*White Mill (ST 957 007)*: A mile and a half south-east of Shapwick, beside a turning on the lane to Pamphill, is an extensive but disused water-driven corn mill on the north bank of the River Stour. An archway over the mill-race has a 1776 keystone but there has been a mill on the site since before the Domesday Book of 1086.

The buildings are two or three storeys with brick walls and tile roofs. Inside there is still machinery and a water-wheel. The Trust's long-term plan is for a restoration project.

*White Mill Bridge (ST 958 006)*: This eight-arched mediaeval bridge, dating from the 1500s and repaired in 1713, is the most graceful in Dorset. There was a bridge here at least as early as 1341 and the amount of stone that has been used is an indication of the former importance of these little-used lanes.

It spans the Stour just downstream from White Mill and though it is owned by the county rather than the Trust it makes a dominant and delightful backdrop to the view across the meadows. The parapet bulges at the cutwaters and the stone is a mix of grey Purbeck ashlars with blocks of brown gritstone from the Dorset heaths. As with a number of Dorset's older bridges it carries a cast-iron plate, from early last century, with the threat that anyone causing damage is liable to seven years' transportation.

*Legend of Knowlton Bell:*

> "Knowlton bell is stole
> And thrown into White Mill Hole
> Where all the devils in hell
> Could never pull up Knowlton bell."

It was stolen from the church, now ruined, close to the B3078 to the south of Cranborne. As the doggerel implies, the bell is believed to contain supernatural powers that prevented its recovery after the thieves dumped it in the mill pond, from the bridge, because they were being pursued.

On the other hand, spoiling a good story, there are alternative traditions that the bell was raised and put into Shapwick or Sturminster Marshall churches or taken away by a man from Horton, Mr Compton. But given this diversity of thought, why believe them? There is every chance that the verse is the correct memory of events, and Knowlton bell did defy lifting attempts and still lies in the riverbed.

*Landscape:* A mixture of lowland pastures and arable fields an alluvial gravels in the Stour valley. The Trust intends to prevent any further removal of hedges as, at Shapwick, many of them preserve boundaries of mediaeval or even pre-Conquest field systems in strips that run at right-angles from the valley lane.

*Trust ownership:* 1,000 acres, part of lands left to the Trust by Ralph Bankes who died in 1981.

*Location and access:* Turn off the B3082, Wimborne to Blandford road, for Shapwick village. The turning is opposite the entrance to Badbury Rings. From Shapwick the lane down the valley, towards Sturminster Marshall, brings you to White Mill and then White Mill Bridge.

**Sharford Bridge**, Corfe Castle - see entry for **Scotland Farm**

**Shedbush Farm**, Stanton St Gabriel - see entry for **Stanton St Gabriel**

**Shell Bay**, Studland - see entry for **Studland Heath National Nature Reserve**

Sherriff - playwright **Robert Cedric Sherriff** [1896-1975] lived at **Downhouse Farm**, Symondsbury. He loved the spot so much that when it came time to leave, in 1966, he gave his 176 acres to the National Trust. For a potted biography of R.C. Sherriff, see under the entry for **Thorncombe Beacon**.

Snyders - for Dutch animal painter **Frans Snyders** [1579-1657] see entry for **Kingston Lacy House**

## SOUTH DOWN FARM, SEA BARN FARM, RINGSTEAD BAY, BURNING CLIFF, and WHITE NOTHE
*the first major headland east of Weymouth*                    *SY 760 823*

*Burning Cliff (SY 762 814)*: The central area above Ringstead Bay, between Rose Cottage and Holworth House, became a tourist attraction for Weymouth visitors when it caught fire in 1826-29. A booklet describing the occurrence was sold nearby at Bagg's Cottage: *Observations on Holworth Cliff, containing Local Particulars illustrative and explanatory of the Extraordinary Phenomenon of Subterraneous Fire, existing within its interior recesses.*

A similar apparent oxidation of iron-pyrites in the oil shales, causing continuous smoking from vent holes in the cliff and temperatures of 500 degrees centigrade, took place at Clavell's Hard, Kimmeridge, in 1973 and burned for months, leaving an area of shale that had been turned from grey to orange in the process. The strong sulphur dioxide fumes induced dizziness.

Not that there's much chance of Burning Cliff living up to its name these days; the hollow between Ringstead and the foothills of White Nothe is now smothered with dense vegetation.

*Smugglers' path (SY 773 808)*: The zig-zag track down the 500 foot chalk headland at White Nothe to the rocky foreshore is a public path but the National Trust say "it is too dangerous for walkers". The narrow grassy path was brought to fame by John Meade Falkner in his Victorian smuggling classic, *Moonfleet*, which is largely set on the Fleet coast on the other side of Weymouth but uses this steep ascent for the climax, the escape scene:

> "Just at the end of this flat ledge, furthest from where the bridle-path leads down, but not a hundred yards from where we stand, there is a sheep-track leading up the cliff. It starts where the under-cliff dies back again into the chalk face, and climbs by slants and elbow-turns up to the top. The shepherds call it the Zigzag, and even sheep lose

South Down Farm reaches the sea at White Nothe: tumbling chalk undercliff of a great headland, overlooking Ringstead Bay and Weymouth Bay from 495 feet, with the old coastguard cottages on top being the highest buildings on the Dorset coast. Photograph: Rodney Legg.

their footing on it; and of men I never heard but one had climbed it, and that was lander Jordan, when the Excise was on his heels, half a century back.

"And 'twas a task that might cow the bravest, and when I looked upon the Zigzag, it seemed better to stay where we were and fall into the hands of the posse than set foot on that awful way, and fall upon the rocks below. For the Zigzag started off as a fair enough chalk path, but in a few paces narrowed down till it was but a whiter thread against the grey-white cliff-face, and afterwards turned sharply back, crossing a hundred feet direct above our heads. And then I smelt an evil stench, and looking about, saw the blown-out carcass of a rotting sheep lie close at hand."

A range of Coastguard Cottages at the top of the cliff, just beyond the Trust's land, are – at 495 feet – the highest inhabited buildings on the Dorset coast. They were built early in the nineteenth century when the era of semi-romantic smuggling was being brought to a close.

*Other literary associations:* The burial place of the ashes of Dorset author Llewelyn Powys lies to the east of the Trust's lands, beneath a four foot block of Portland stone between the two concrete obelisks that line-up as navigation marks to show the deep water channel into Portland Harbour.

The gravestone was cut by Elizabeth Muntz and inscribed: "Llewelyn Powys. 3 August 1884, 2 December 1939. The living. The living. He shall praise thee." Powys insisted that White Nothe should be called the White Nose, because of its profile, and it is called "White Nothe or White Nose" on the 6-inch Ordnance map of 1903, though these days "White Nose" has become a lost cause.

*Landscape:* The Trust owns almost all the foreshore and craggy landslipped undercliff from Ringstead eastward to White Nothe, the 500 foot headland that is the western extremity of the coastal chalklands in Dorset. Inland from the pebble beach the Trust has pastoral fringes around the thatched Sea Barn and a slab of cereal lands that extend to the foot of the escarpment at Bascombe Barn and Moigns Down.

*Trust ownership:* 454 acres; the 273-acre South Down Farm was transferred by the Treasury through the National Land Fund in 1949 and the remaining 107 acres of undercliff were bought with Enterprise Neptune funds in 1968. 74 acres at Sea Barn Farm were added in 1984 through various bequests and grants.

*Location and access:* Turn south off the A353 Weymouth to Wareham road between Osmington and Warmwell Cross roundabout. The turning, at Upton, is beside a wood. A two mile lane leads to the Trust's car-park, on the crest of a down overlooking the sea. Paths are signposted to the Burning Cliff and Ringstead Bay [half a mile] and uphill on to the top of White Nothe [a mile].

**Southover**, Burton Bradstock - see entry for **Burton Cliff**

## THE SPITTLES

*immediately east of Lyme Regis*                                    *SY 350 930*

*The Lyme Volcano:* This was the tag given to the 1908 spontaneous combustion that started in the oily shales that overlie the blue lias boulders. The cliff smouldered away for several years, though its later life was said to have been prolonged by cartloads of coal courtesy of Lyme traders who did not wish to lose their tourist attraction. The Trust owns another Burning Cliff, at Ringstead Bay [*see entry for South Down Farm*].

*The name:* Spittles is among the most descriptive names on the Dorset coast, the mudflows appearing as if they were spat out from the cliff. Disappointingly, the researched origin of the name is that the middle English 'spitel' was land on which a hospital was built - unlikely in this case - or land owned by a hospital.

*Landscape:* Cracking meadows and landslipped undercliff. The eastern end of the Spittles, next to Black Ven, was carried across the Canary Ledges and into the sea by mudflows in 1959 and 1969-70.

Other parts of the cliff have edged towards the sea in recent years, the slippage being caused by rainfall seeping down through the chert and greensand top layers which then slide off the underlying liassic clays. The area is leased by the National Trust to the Dorset Trust for Nature Conservation.

*Trust ownership:* 126 acres, bought with Enterprise Neptune funds in 1974.

*Location and access:* Park in Lyme Regis. Where the south-west coast footpath leaves the town on the east side, opposite the cemetery, it skirts above The Spittles. This, and any path in the cliff area, is liable to diversion or closure in the event of further landslides. Do not venture on to an active mudflow.

**Spread Eagle Hill**, Melbury Abbas - see entry for **Melbury Beacon**

## STANTON ST GABRIEL, SHEDBUSH FARM, NORCHARD FARM, FILCOMBE FARM, and LANGDON HILL
*south of Morcombelake*                                          *SY 401 924*

*St Gabriel's Church (SY 402 924)*: Thirteenth century lias-stone ruin. Services were last held before 1800. It still stands, as a roofless shell, in its own parish, as a reminder that the nearby thatched cottage and farmhouse used to be part of a dense cluster of buildings in the valley beneath Golden Cap.

After the French wars the church was "frequently used as a receiving house for smuggled kegs of brandy".

The porch and walls of the rectangular single-cell church were capped and restored to their present reasonably impressive state, after years of neglect, following acquisition by the National Trust in 1967.

*Stanton St Gabriel (SY 400 924)*: There are few buildings now but in 1650 twenty-three families were living around the green. The surviving thatched cottages are let by the Trust for self-catering holidays. "Please remember to feed the badger" is on the list of instructions.

*Shedbush Farm (SY 405 934)*: Typical yellow-stone and thatch buildings of a small west Dorset dairy farm, forming an unusually complete collection and dating from 1700.

*Beach access, on foot:* From Stanton St Gabriel, down the valley to St Gabriel's Mouth. Descend a steep gully. Offshore is St Gabriel's Ledge. You venture down there at your own risk. Do not explore any further as there is no other path up from the sea between Charmouth and Seatown.

*Landscape:* Small fields and dense hedgerows, tall and overhanging, of a nineteenth century mixed farming landscape that has been preserved by the Trust. These are lush herb-rich meadows on a clay soil. Some of the hedges reached house-height in 1985 though they were then cut and laid.

Nowhere else in Dorset is unimproved pastureland still farmed on this scale. It is a most remarkable valley, caught in a time-warp. There are also coppices and larger pine woods, Monument Copse and Langdon Hill, which are under-stood with holly. The views are of Lyme Regis and Golden Cap, which dominates the scene and has its own entry.

**Stanton St Gabriel, near Chideock: the approach to Norchard Farm in the Trust-owned valley beneath Golden Cap. Photograph: Colin Graham.**

Stanton St Gabriel: its church and farmhouse were once the hub of a thriving community at the heart of this west Dorset coastal valley. Photograph: Colin Graham.

*Trust ownership:* 505 acres, bought in 1967-72 with Enterprise Neptune funds and legacies from Miss Jessie McNab, R.I. Gunn, and Miss Gwendolen Pelly.

*Location and access:* South of the A35 between Lyme Regis and Bridport. Seaward of Morcombelake. Turn off the A35 between Morcombelake and Chideock, at the top of Chideock Hill, into Muddyford Lane. Then turn immediately left and then right into the trees. There is a car-park at the end in the wood on Langdon Hill. Walk back along the lane and then turn left, to Stanton St Gabriel. It is a mile walk. Paths branch off to the farms and you can return to Langdon Hill from the cliff footpath, via Golden Cap.

On returning to the main road be very careful how you enter the fast traffic on this hill-top dual carriageway.

**Stanton St Gabriel** parish - see entries for **Golden Cap/ St Wite's Well and Ship Farm/ Stanton St Gabriel, Shedbush Farm, and Norchand Farm/** and **Stonebarrow Hill, Cain's Folly, Chardown Hill, Westhay Farm, and Upcot Farm**

**Steeple** parish - see entry for **Creech Grange Arch, known locally as Bond's Folly**

Stephen - for **King Stephen** [?1097-1154] see entries for **Corfe Castle** and **Corfe Common (The Rings)**

**Stinsford** parish - see entry for **Hardy's Cottage Birthplace**

## STONEBARROW HILL, CAIN'S FOLLY, CHARDOWN HILL, NEWLANDS BATCH, WESTHAY FARM, and UPCOT FARM
*east of Charmouth* SY 385 935

*Ichthyosaur:* One of the largest fossil skeletons ever found in Britain of this dolphin-like dinosaur, which lived on cuttlefish and squid, was discovered in the late 1980s on the cliffs between Charmouth and Stanton St Gabriel (*SY 370 930*). It comprised a twenty-five foot body section, including six foot of skull, but lacked what would have been a further ten feet of tail. It has a pointed snout, razor-like teeth, and a series of what seem to have been moveable plates along the

**Stonebarrow Hill, above Charmouth: an extended family gathers around the trough, as the mist rises from the valley. Photograph: Colin Graham.**

top of the backbone. The creature had sunk into the limy mud of the shallow sub-tropical Lower Jurassic sea about 200 million years ago and reappeared among bands of what are now blue lias shale and limestone eroding at the cliff-edge. The National Heritage Memorial Fund made a grant of £8,000 to help Bristol Museum and Art Gallery acquire this important specimen [1989].

*Ancient trackway:* The track across the top of Stonebarrow Hill, beside which the Trust has established a picnic area, was the main road from Charmouth to Morcombelake until it was replaced by the northern turnpike [the present A35, until completion of the Charmouth by-pass] in 1824. It was the main Dorchester to Exeter coach road and seems to be on the course of the 'lost' Roman road between the two towns.

*Wartime radar station (SY 378 930):* On the undercliff, 150 feet below Cain's Folly cliff-edge, visible only from the top. It slipped down the cliff in a landslip on 14 May 1942, to the surprise of the RAF crew who are reputed to have been inside at the time, and who stepped out when it came to a halt at the bottom.

*Post-war radar station (SY 383 934):* At the centre of Stonebarrow Hill, behind a high security fence, relinquished by the Ministry of Defence in 1978 and used by the Trust as an information point and base for work parties.

*Names:* Stonebarrow must have been an ancient cairn, but it has disappeared in all probability in order to fill ruts in the road.

Cain's Folly is recorded as the name of the landslipped wood, but sounds as if it must have been coined originally for a building that went the same way.

Westhay Farm is Old English, meaning simply 'west enclosure', and Upcot is just as easy - 'upper house'.

*Landscape:* Chert-topped plateau of upper greensand, prone to gorse scrub on the south side but heavily wooded on the damper northern slopes [Newlands Batch]. The seaward end of this mile-long 500-foot high ridge is known as Cain's Folly, the name being last applied to a beech clump that went over the cliff in 1942.

Here the wartime radar station lies tilting in a trough but other parts of the thousand-foot wide undercliff came down in 1877. The sliding gault clays brought with them a hundred and fifty feet of upper greensand and chert, which comprise the walkable top of the headland. This cliff

Stonebarrow Hill falls into the sea at Cain's Folly: literally so, as with this wartime radar station which slipped over the edge in 1942. Photograph: Colin Graham.

edge has receded by four hundred feet since the 1860s but the loss of the undercliff into the sea is at a much slower rate, of just over a hundred feet in the same period.

The sea views are to Start Point and Golden Cap. Inland there are the Trust-owned peaks of Lambert's Castle, Pilsdon Pen and Lewesdon, with Hardown Hill nearer and to the right. The Trust's immediately adjacent lands extend along the ridge to Chardown Hill and downhill to the small pastures around Westhay and Upcot Farms.

*Trust ownership:* 771 acres, of which 274 acres at Stonebarrow Hill and Westhay Farm were the starting point for the Trust's Golden Cap estate, being given in 1961 in memory of Oliver Morland. The remainder was acquired in 1966 with Enterprise Neptune funds, except for 61 acres which were added in 1978-81 through a variety of appeal funds and a legacy from Miss S.W. St Paul.

*Location and access:* Stonebarrow is the hill immediately east of Charmouth, to the south of the A35 between Lyme Regis and Bridport. It is climbed by Stonebarrow Lane, which starts beside the Newlands Hotel, but drive slowly and cautiously. It is narrow, winding and dangerous. Sound your horn at corners and prepare to encounter walkers trapped between cars or obscured by the high banks. At the top you cross a cattle-grid into the Trust's picnic area car-park.


**Stourpaine** parish - see entry for **Hod Hill**


**Straw Barrow**, Shapwick - see listing for **Badbury area finds** and **Badbury Rings** main entry


**Studland Castle (lost)**, Studland - see entry for **Old Harry Rocks**


**STUDLAND HEATH NATIONAL NATURE RESERVE including GOD-LINGSTON HEATH, THE AGGLESTONE, PUCKSTONE, LITTLE SEA, SHELL BAY, THE TRAINING BANK, BRAMBLE BUSH BAY, and REDHORN QUAY**
*north and west of Studland*                                     *SZ 020 830*

*Geology:* Outcrops of dark-red iron-impregnated sandstone of the Bagshot beds are the eroded remains of a layer of rock that once covered the sands and clays of the heath. These remnants lie on steep-sided hillocks between shallow valleys filled with peat.

*Agglestone (SZ 022 828):* The greatest of the natural boulders that outcrop on Godlingston and Studland Heath, north-west of Studland. Being the biggest, the Agglestone inspired a mass of folklore.

The name itself has roots in the supernatural and probably means *hagolstan,* the Old English for 'hailstone', suggesting that it was thought to have fallen from the sky. Charles Warne, a nineteenth century antiquary, wrote of the Agglestone:

> The country people say of it that his Satanic majesty (who is often a very important personage in these capricious parts) was one day sitting on the Needles Rock, Isle of Wight, whence, espying Corfe Castle in the distance, he took the cap from his head and threw it across the sea, with the intent of demolishing that structure. But it would appear that he had over-estimated his powers of jactation, for the missile fell short of its mark; and there it stands to this day on Studland Heath, a monument of disappointed malice, a wonder to the peasantry, and a theme of antiquarian conjecture.

The conjecture ended long ago when geologists explained that the Agglestone was in no way mysterious and had not been taken to Studland Heath by a glacier, the devil, prehistoric man or anything else.

It was a single great stone about sixteen feet high, twice that in diameter, and weighing about four hundred tons. It became a natural wonder of Purbeck because of its anvil-shape and grand position on a sandy hill overlooking Studland Bay and Poole Harbour. These words are in the past tense because the stone took a tumble in September 1970 and collapsed on its side, which does have the advantage that with a great deal of care it is now (physically) possible to climb to the top.

*Puckstone (SZ 021 831):* Another outcrop of dark-red iron-impregnated sandstone, being further remains of a layer which once covered the softer sands and clays of the Bagshot beds, between Godlingston Heath and Studland Heath.

It takes its name from *puca,* meaning 'goblin'. Such rocks were regarded as having supernatural origins and have gathered a cluster of folk-tales.

*Landforms:* The great sandy beaches of Studland and Shell Bay grow into wide dunes that enclose on the South Haven Peninsula [east of the Ferry Road] a remarkable freshwater lagoon, the Little Sea.

Studland National Nature Reserve: beach-huts being inundated by the sand dunes of one of the best beaches in England, facing east towards the shallow waters of Studland Bay and Poole Bay and generally out of the prevailing wind. Photograph: Colin Graham.

Studland National Nature Reserve: geology at the Agglestone, featuring the iron-impregnated gritstone of the Bagshot beds, which once capped these sandy knolls. Photograph: Colin Graham.

Studland National Nature Reserve: the Puckstone, seen from the south-east, amongst heather and gorse, with the conifer plantations of the Rempstone Estate marking the boundary of the Trust lands a mile away. Photograph: Colin Graham.

*Little Sea (SZ 030 845)*: Dating from 1700 to 1850, before that being an arm of the open sea. Dune build-up cut off its tidal channel, which was the outlet from the north-east of the lake, and created a freshwater lagoon. The channel can still be traced as alternating patches of marshland and carr scrub. When the Ordnance Survey re-surveyed the beach east of Little Sea in 1959 they found the high water mark had jumped fifty yards out to sea in only five years. Eels are common in the Little Sea and rarely it has otters. The frequent visitors are heron, fishing for palmate newts. Dabchick are also there in the summer, being the only grebes to breed in Purbeck, but it is winter when it attracts flocks of waterfowl. These include garganey, gadwall, goldeneye, common scoter, scaup, mute swan and whooper swan. Redpoll breed in the surrounding birch clumps.

*Salt pans (SZ 026 857)*: Between Jerry's Point and Redhorn Quay, on the Poole Harbour shore towards Brand's Bay, there are seventy-one salt-pans and another six between Brand's Ford and Greenland. Each is a depression about twenty feet across, slightly dished and surrounded by a circular bank about a foot high. There is no evidence to suggest their date but they are probably either Roman or mediaeval. One group has an associated batch of sandy mounds.

*Boundary stones (SZ 027 852)*: Six stones, now fallen, are in a line along the centre of the South Haven Peninsula, near the site of the demolished Curlew Cottages to the east of the Ferry Road. Their function is unknown.

*Bramble Bush Bay (SZ 030 860)*: The inlet southwards from Gravel Point on the harbour side of the South Haven Peninsula has had moorings for houseboats since before the Great War.

*Redhorn Quay (SZ 021 855)*: Disused ancient jetty at the north-east corner of Brand's Bay, the traditional crossing point from Poole to the South Haven Peninsula before the road was opened to its northern tip — which was only a narrow spit in mediaeval times. Old blocks of granite, however, are not part of any jetty. They seem to have been ballast dumped by Cornish craft.

*Stone and clay-pits (SZ 015 827)*: The central parts of Godlingston Heath were dug in the Middle Ages and until the nineteenth century for the brown gritstone or carr-stone, now more generally called heathstone, which can be seen in many of the farm buildings to the north of Purbeck Hills. It is often mixed with grey Purbeck stone in some of the grander buildings of east Dorset including Wimborne Minster. There are traces of claypits in the north-west corner of the heath, the boundary of which is now the conifer plantation of the Rempstone Estate.

*The Training Bank (SZ 041 861 to SZ 048 851):* From the east side of Shell Bay a man-made spit of rocks can be followed for more than half a mile into Poole Harbour at low tide. This was constructed in the 1930s and holds the sands back from the Swash Channel approach to the harbour entrance.

*Project Fougasse:* Being three miles long, gently shelving and usually sheltered, the beaches of Studland Bay and Shell Bay were particularly vulnerable to Hitler's threatened Operation Sealion when England faced invasion in 1940. As well as the usual defences of anti-tank scaffolding, barbed wire, minefields and pill-boxes, Studland was selected for special attention with a refinement that the Germans feared most.

Oil pipes were laid across Studland Beach and around Redend Point for Project Fougasse, an anti-invasion measure in which the sea was set on fire.

Tests were watched from Redend Point on 20 December 1940 by General Harold Alexander, General Officer Commanding-in-Chief of Southern Command, and Major-General Bernard Montgomery of 5th Corps. It was a successful daytime demonstration but the sea became too choppy for the intended repeat performance after dark. "Nazis assured of a warm welcome" had been the intended propaganda headline.

When the full-scale test was eventually ignited, breaking the blackout regulations on the night of 1 February 1941, the light from Studland was so intense that it was said you could read a newspaper in Bournemouth Square.

*Mountbatten's commandos:* Studland and Shell Bay beaches were cleared of their anti-invasion scaffolding and mines in January 1943 to provide a training area for the commandos of Combined Operations. They were based in Poole under the command of Acting Admiral Louis Mountbatten who had his country house headquarters at Anderson Manor, near Bere Regis.

*Exercise Smash:* The liveliest days of Studland's war - see next entry [*and that for Fort Henry, listed under Old Harry Rocks*].

*Studland Assault Training Beach:* Exercise Smash hit Studland beach in April 1944 as the live-fire rehearsal for the forthcoming invasion of Normandy. Studland's wide sands duplicated the D-Day beachheads.

To provide additional touches of reality there was a massive use of live ammunition throughout the attack on Studland, ranging from small-arms to bombardments with rockets and bombs.

Troops poured ashore from assault landing craft, including the 1st Battalion of the Dorsetshire Regiment who returned to their native heath. Tank landing craft unleashed amphibious armoured cars and Stuart light tanks which waded ashore in up to six feet of water, a pair of funnels carrying air to the engine and then disposing of the exhaust fumes.

Another wave of Valentine Duplex-driven tanks swam ashore with huge skirts keeping them afloat. Or at least in theory, for several had mishaps in being launched from the landing craft or ploughing through the waves. Seven sank to the bottom of Poole Bay.

On land, at the dunes, "Hobart's Funnies" progressed from initial derision to full admiration. Churchill tanks were unable to push their way through the sands. Then Major-General Percy Hobart of the 79th Armoured Division demonstrated his AVRE, which was a Heath Robinson contraption bolted on top of a tank, with a huge drum unwinding carpet from a bobbin. This went under the tracks and was laid across the soft sands. Normal Churchill tanks then drove up the carpet and successfully crossed the dunes.

All this activity was monitored from a massive concrete bunker, the Fort Henry observation post on Redend Point [*see entry for Old Harry Rocks*], a row of field glasses lined the eighty feet long observation slit. Field commanders, American as well as British, were joined by a succession of top brass, including Churchill, Eisenhower and Montgomery.

The assault exercise area was protected, from December 1943 to June 1944, by the 184th Auxiliary Anti-Aircraft Gun Battalion of the First United States Army.

*Ukrainian clear-up:* As a result of the live-fire exercises in 1943-45, Studland Heath was littered with discarded and unexploded ammunition. Warning signs were everywhere until late in the 1950s.

Though the credit for blowing up piles of munitions at Studland was usually given to the Royal Marines, the physical act of collection was carried out by a band of fearless Ukrainian exiles who collected shells for their value as scrap-metal. Because of the soft sands, the beach and dunes had a level of unexploded devices of unprecedented proportions. Mine-detectors were used and then the Ukrainians dug out their finds.

This operation extended over many summers. Initially, the Ukrainians offered their services for this dangerous work in 1945, when the alternative was a flight home to Odessa and a bullet in the back of the head from Uncle Joe.

*Landscape:* The interesting ecology of the heath is not on the conspicuous drier crests but in the pockets of acid bog. Here amongst the sphagnum grow highly specialised species. *Erica ciliaris* is the "Dorset Heath", and grows only in Purbeck and the Pyrenees. It thrives here with the blue marsh gentian, insectivorous sundews, tufts of cotton grass, and the burnt orchid.

Look out for colourful dragonflies, and green woodpeckers ("yaffles" these are called in Dorset) which fly out of the sallow scrub fringing the heath.

The sandier parts are mainly notable for the smooth snake (*Coronella austriaca*) and its sand lizard prey (*Lacerta agilis agilis*) which are now on the point of extinction from most other areas of their specialised heathland habitat. Ironically the first British record for the smooth snake came in 1859 from what is now the Bournemouth International Centre. Though harmless it was common enough to be killed there in scores in the 1868 drought. It is now fully protected by law.

Stonechats nest in the dense old heather. The cocky purple-breasted Dartford warbler prefers the gorse scrub, or "vurze" as it is in the Dorset tongue. The changing fortunes of this bird and these wild lands are described in my book on *Purbeck's Heath* [1987].

*Trust ownership:* 1,800 acres, 1,500 of which are leased to the Nature Conservancy Council [English Nature] for a National Nature Reserve. This was established in 1962 and extended later. Part of the Corfe Castle Estate left to the Trust by Ralph Bankes on his death in 1981.

*Location and access:* Studland is approached from Corfe Castle by the B3351 or from the north, across the mouth of Poole Harbour, by a pay-ferry from Sandbanks at Poole. There are large beach car-parks at Studland; the Knoll car-park has the capacity for 1,700 cars. There is also parking at Shell Bay and in a viewpoint layby beside the B3351 a short distance west of the Isle of Purbeck Golf Course.

Public paths lead across the heath from the east side of the Golf Course. The western one is to the north-west corner of Godlingston Heath. The centre one crosses the middle of the heath. The eastern one goes to Studland with an offshoot to the Agglestone, one mile into the heath.

The Agglestone can also be reached from Studland, west from the start of the Ferry Road between Studland Bay House and the Knoll House Hotel.

Coastal paths follow the edge of the dunes and run close to the shores of Poole Harbour. This is the busiest place in Dorset at the height of the summer, with all the car-parks filling early and at some weekends police road-blocks to prevent any more visitors approaching from Corfe Castle.

It is a nature reserve with some human naturists in the warmer weather. The Trust's 1986 management plan comments: "The use of the central section of Studland Bay by nudists will be accepted but every effort made through an increased wardening presence to persuade naturists to remain within accepted boundaries on the beach. Regular liaison will be maintained with the police."

**Studland Manor Hotel**, Studland - see entry for **Studland Village**

**Studland** parish - see **Brownsea Island/ Ballard Down Obelisk** (listed under **Godlingston Hill**)**/ Kingswood Barrows and Fishing Barrows Group/ The Pinnacle, King Barrow, Studland Castle (lost), Parson's Barn, Fort Henry, Ballard Cliff, and Manor Farm/ Studland Heath National Nature Reserve including Godlingston Heath, the Agglestone, Puckstone, Little Sea, Shell Bay, the Training Bank, Bramble Bush Bay, and Redhorn Quay/ Studland Village, Saxon cross-base, Studland Manor Hotel, Bankes Arms Hotel, Cliff End, and Knoll House Grounds/ and Woodhouse Hill** (listed under **Wilkswood Farm**)

## STUDLAND VILLAGE, SAXON CROSS-BASE, STUDLAND MANOR HOTEL, BANKES ARMS HOTEL, CLIFF END, and KNOLL HOUSE GROUNDS

*north of Swanage*          *SZ 035 824*

*Studland village:* Though surrounded by the Bankes estate the parish church had remained in the advowson - patronage, being the right to appoint the rector - of the Pleydell family since the seventeenth century. Despite that the church inevitably had strong Bankes connections and the items that follow mention some of these.

St Nicholas's Church is enthusiastically described by Fred Pitfield in his *Purbeck Parish Churches* [1985] as "the oldest surviving complete church in Dorset". Its Saxon origins and the quality and extent of the Norman work show that Studland started life as a place of some importance. Fortunately, for the survival of the church, it was to stay a village. In other places the churches expanded with the population but in Studland "its ancient church has survived practically in its original state". Note the magnificent mid-twelfth century internal tower arch and the south doorway. There are also Norman windows, bowl-shaped font, corbel-table heads, and moulded capitals. An unexpected early treasure is a Coptic processional cross from sixth century Egypt though that came as a gift from a parishioner. The inscription is partly decipherable: "This is the cross of ... Blessed be his seed. Who gave it to Mary, the daughter of ..."

Romano-British stone-lined graves have been found in the church-yard, including that of a decapitated woman. She was dug up in 1951 and now resides in the Red House Museum, Christchurch. Her head had been taken off after death, probably in the belief that this would still a restless spirit.

Studland therefore shows the conversion of a pagan sacred site into that for a Christian Saxon church.

*Memorials to Cornet Bankes VC:* A stained glass window in Studland church and an inscription on the Bankes family tomb in the churchyard record the heroism of Cornet Bankes. He was the son of the late George Bankes MP of Kingston Lacy but his memorials are here because he preferred the Studland end of the estate and had a passion for sailing.

Cornet Bankes was killed during the Indian Mutiny. He went to India in 1857, at the age of twenty-one, as a subaltern in the 7th Hussars. The Times correspondent, William Howard Russell, would tell the world of his courage in repelling a rebel charge at the end of the British siege of their stronghold at Lucknow, on 19 March 1858:

"A band of Ghazees, who issued out of an old mud fort and charged the guns and the party of the 7th Hussars covering them, had got the lad down and hacked at him in that cruel way until he was rescued by his comrades. It is perfectly astonishing, to witness his cheerfulness and resignation."

"If I get out of this, Russell", the fatally wounded young man said, "They tell me I'll be able to go yachting, and that's all I care about. We'll have many a jolly cruise together." He paused for a moment: "If it please God."

Cornet Bankes was dying in the hospital of the 53rd Regiment in the Indian Imam Bara temple-palace at Lucknow. Russell described his injuries as frightful:

"One leg lopped off above the knee, one arm cut off, the other leg nearly severed, the other arm cut through the bone, and several cuts on the body."

Whilst lying there he heard that Sir Colin Campbell had recommended him for the Victoria Cross. Cornet Bankes died on 6 April 1858 and was buried in the churchyard of the ruined cantonment church that stood close to the camp of the 7th Hussars. The posthumous award of the Victoria Cross would be confirmed by the Queen and presented by her to Bankes's widowed mother at Kingston Lacy.

*Gravestone of Sergeant William Lawrence*: A stone in the churchyard at Studland sets out the graphic military career of Waterloo veteran Sergeant William Lawrence who retired from the 40th Regiment of Foot to keep the Duke of Wellington public house [now the Bankes Arms Hotel] and died at the age of seventy-eight:

"To the honoured memory of Serjeant William Lawrence (of the 40th Regiment Foot) who after a long and eventful life in the service of his country peacefully ended his days at Studland November 11th 1869. He served with his distinguished regiment in the war in South America 1805 and through the whole of the Peninsula War 1808-1813. He received a silver medal and no less than ten clasps for the battles in which he was engaged - Roleia, Vimiera, Talavera, Ciudad Rodrigo, Badajoz (in which desperate assault being one of the volunteers for the forlorn hope he was most severely wounded), Vittoria, Pyrenees, Nivells, Orthes, Toulouse. He also fought at the glorious victory of

Studland Village on the Purbeck coast: 1976 cross, carved by Purbeck marbler Treleven Haysom on the theme of 'Spaceship Earth'. It is set on a Saxon heathstone plinth, which had lost its shaft, and stands beside the lane leading to St Nicholas Church. Photograph: Colin Graham.

Waterloo June 18th 1815.

"Whilst still serving with his Regiment during the Occupation of Paris by the Allied Armies Serjeant Lawrence married Clotilde Clairet at St. Germain-en-Laye who died Septr. 26th 1853 and was buried beneath this Spot."

They have one of the best biographical gravestones in Europe.

*Saxon cross-base (SZ 036 824)*: The heathstone block, four feet in diameter, at the base of the 1970s Celtic-style cross beside the lane leading to the church is the only surviving part of a mediaeval preaching cross in the Isle of Purbeck. Its modern Purbeck stone top has Saxon type scroll work though it incorporates clues to its date — such as a Concorde airliner.

*Studland Manor Hotel (SZ 037 827)*: The estate's marine villa, which was built by George Bankes MP [died 1856] and used by his sons, including Cornet who is mentioned above, as the base for their sailing adventures into the Channel.

It may incorporate earlier walls and the general contrived irregularity includes two round towers, on the north-west side, which could have been inspired by the lost Studland Castle at Old Harry Rocks.

Inside, the building has re-used fittings such as a Gothic landing, a fine eighteenth century carved fireplace, and a door surround featuring Orpheus in the forest with the wild animals.

*Bankes Arms Hotel (SZ 037 825)*: Formerly the Duke of Wellington and then the New Inn. A modern re-building of the stone-roofed cottage that used to form a rustic setting on the back lane just above the little chine that opens on to Studland's offshore beach, the one south-east of Redend Point.

From the 1820s to the 1850s, as the Duke of Wellington, it was kept by William Lawrence, the Waterloo veteran whose exploits are set out above.

*Cliff End (SZ 038 825)*: Here a promising 38-year-old mathematician named Bertrand Russell first went to bed with Lady Ottoline Morrell, the wife of Liberal MP Philip Morrell, during the Easter of 1911.

The affair lasted until 1916 when Russell was thrown out of Trinity College for his opposition to the Great War. Bertrand became the third Earl Russell in 1931, on the death of his elder brother, and is remembered as an anti-nuclear campaigner and a philosopher.

His Studland interlude was spent at Cliff End, a house in the trees between the Bankes Arms Hotel and the small beach that lies to the south-east of Redend Point.

*Knoll House grounds (SZ 031 833):* Knoll House was built on Knowl Hill in the 1920s by the thirteenth Duke of Hamilton [1862-1940] as his summer home.

His son, the fourteenth Duke [1903-73], had his name borrowed in 1941 by MI6, for a lengthy correspondence with Hitler's deputy Rudolf Hess, which caused his defection to the Duke's Scottish estate on 11 May that year, thinking he could make peace with an anti-Churchill faction.

Knoll House is now an hotel. Its buildings and gardens are on a parcel of land bought from the Bankes estate but the grounds are leased from the National Trust.

*Heinkel crash:* A German Heinkel He111 bomber (call-sign G1 + BH), one of a massed force of 220 enemy aircraft that attacked the British Aeroplane Company's works at Filton on 25 September 1940, was intercepted on its way home by Hurricanes of 238 Squadron. They brought it down over Studland.

The pilot was able to steer it to a crash-landing at Westfield Farm. All five crewmen were injured, four of them not seriously, but the flight mechanic died half and hour later.

By this time wine waiter Theo Janku had taken the Germans prisoner with the aid of an unloaded Home Guard rifle and relieved them of their Lugers. On seeing there were casualties the Studland villagers then tried to help the Germans and provided cigarettes and tea.

"This is war, not a bloody pepershow," a sentry from the Suffolk Regiment told onlookers as he guarded the aircraft. It was salvaged and reassembled for Cardiff's war weapons week.

*Landscape:* Studland is a scattering of cottages and later houses on a wooded rise between three hundred and a thousand yards inland from Redend Point at the south-west corner of Studland Bay.

The Trust owns Studland's little village green, which is registered (VG37, 0.11 hectares) and, if anything, has been enhanced by the adjoining and characterful 1990-built brick houses that have actually benefited from having an architect.

The village and its paddocks are fringed on the northern side by heathland, to the east by sandy cliffs fifty feet or so in height, and on the southern extremity by rolling chalklands.

*Trust ownership:* 500 acres, part of the Corfe Castle Estate left to the Trust by Ralph Bankes in 1982.

*Location and access:* Use the beach car-parks, off the B3351 – the road from Corfe Castle – rather than try to park in the narrow lanes. Get there early if you are coming on a hot day at the height of summer.

Sturt – for landowner **Humphrey Sturt** [1725-86] see entry for **Brownsea Island**

**Swanage** parish – see entries for **Belle Vue Cliffs/ Godlingston Manor, Godlingston Hill, Ulwell Gap/ Godlingston Wood** (listed under **Wilkswood Farm**)/ **Verney Farm/** and **Whitecliff Farm, Ballard Down, and Punfield Cove**

**Symondsbury** parish – see entry for **Thorncombe Beacon, Downhouse Farm, Doghouse Hill**

**Talbot's Wood**, Langton Matravers – see entry for **Wilkswood Farm**

**THORNCOMBE BEACON, DOWNHOUSE FARM, and DOGHOUSE HILL**

*west of Bridport*                                    *SY 440 915*

*Barrows (SY 436 916 and 437 917):* Three Bronze Age burial mounds, two of them on the Trust's lands, lie between Down House and Thorncombe Beacon.

*Beacon (SY 435 914):* There is a mediaeval and Elizabethan beacon site, as its name suggests, on the Thorncombe Beacon clifftop, It has a 1988 cast-iron fire-holder to commemorate the defeat of the 1588 Spanish Armada.

*Pillbox [site of]:* A World War Two underground shelter on Thorncombe Beacon, either as part of the anti-invasion defences or connected with the secret radar stations that operated along this coast, was regarded as an eyesore and blown up by the Trust. Toads used to live in it.

*Literary associations:* The playwright Robert Cedric Sherriff [1896-1975] lived at Downhouse Farm (*SY 441 918*) and gave it, including the great cliff at Thorncombe Beacon, to the National Trust.

His first performance, in aid of a school chapel restoration fund [1921], led to a professional career that started with *Journey's End,* which was produced in London at the Savoy Theatre [1929]. The works that followed included *Badger's Green* [1930], *Windfall* [1933], *St Helena* [1934], *Miss Mabel* [1948], *Home at Seven* [1950], *The White Carnation* [1953], *The Long Sunset,* [1955], *The Telescope* [1957], *A Shred of Evidence* [1960]. He went into television with *The Ogburn Story* [1963] but had long before established his reputation as a scriptwriter for the big screen, with *The Invisible Man* [1933], *Goodbye Mr Chips* [1936], *The Four Feathers* [1938], *Lady Quartet* [1948], *No Highway* [1950] and *The Dam Busters* [1955]. He never reached quite the same peaks with his novels, but here too the output was substantial, with *The Fortnight in September* [1931], *Greengates* [1936], *The Hopkins Manuscript* [1939], *Chedworth* [1944], *Another Year* [1946], *King John's Treasure* [1954] and *The Wells of St Mary's* [1961]. His autobiography was *No Leading Lady* [1968].

*Landscape:* Expansive vistas of Lyme Bay and the Chesil Beach from Thorncombe Beacon which is a 508-foot high chert-topped plateau. It is one of the great Dorset cliffs and is particularly steep on the side facing Bridport. The Great Ebb and other ledges break the surf at its foot.

Doghouse Hill is also some climb, at 400 feet, but represents no more than the eastern foothills to Thorncombe Beacon.

*Trust ownership:* 230 acres. Downhouse Farm and Thorncombe Beacon were given to the Trust by R.C. Sherriff in 1966. 54 acres at Doghouse Hill were added to the holding through the Enterprise Neptune appeal in 1967.

*Location and access:* South of the A35 to the west of Bridport. The ascent of Thorncombe Beacon is along the coastal footpath, uphill from the east [Eype Mouth, a mile of tough climbing] or from the west [Seatown, just over a mile but not quite so steep]. Eype Mouth is reached by lanes from Bridport – turn west from South Street at the Brewery.

Seatown is reached from Chideock. Turn south off the A35 in the centre of the village, opposite the church, and drive the length of Sea Hill Lane. Take to the coastal path at the end, uphill out of the car-park.

Titian – for Italian painter **Vecelli Tiziano, known as Titian** [1477-1576] see entry for **Kingston Lacy House**

## TOLPUDDLE MARTYRS' TREE and VILLAGE GREEN
*in Tolpuddle*                                            SY 791 944

*The Tolpuddle Martyrs* (or Dorsetshire Labourers, or the Dorchester Unionists as they were known at the time): The following sequence of events gives a potted history of the part in their story that relates to the aged sycamore tree in the centre of the village of Tolpuddle –

*1833, late summer.* Following evening discussions under the sycamore tree on the village green, workers in Tolpuddle form a Friendly Society of Agricultural Labourers. They met in the upstairs of Thomas Standfield's cottage [east side of the filling station] in the main street. The Whig government and supporters of the previous Tory administration unite in apprehension at the spread of industrial trades unionism from the northern towns and London into the shire counties. Lord Melbourne, the Home Secretary, has been warned by Sir Robert Peel that such unions are "the most formidable difficulty and danger" which the country is facing. Melbourne, who admits that in general his maxim is "when in doubt what should be done, do nothing", has received urgent requests for action from Dorset magistrate James Frampton of Moreton House. [Charles Wollaston visited Moreton during the Captain Swing riots of 1830 and found the house "barricaded like an Irish mansion".]

*1833, October.* Mr and Mrs Whetman, who have a paint shop in Dorchester, have been approached by James Loveless of Tolpuddle with designs of "Death" and a skeleton which he requires painting six feet high with the words "Remember Thine End". [Mr Whetman refused; the painting was done elsewhere.]

*1834, 22 February.* A cautionary notice has been posted in the Tolpuddle area warning that "mischieving and designing persons" are inducing labourers to "enter into illegal societies or unions, to which they bind themselves by unlawful oaths". The magistrates state that such activity or persuasion "to become a member of such societies" will render such persons "guilty of felony and liable to be transported for seven years".

*1834, 24 February, 6 am.* Tolpuddle at dawn. The arrest of 37-year-old George Loveless takes place while he is on his way to work in the fields. It is carried out by a constable, James Brine.

Brine – "I have a warrant for you, from the magistrates."

Loveless – "What is its contents, sir?"

Brine – "Take it yourself, you can read it as well as I can." [Loveless reads the charge: that he administered an unlawful oath.]

Brine – "Are you willing to go to the magistrate with me?"

Loveless – "To any place wherever you wish me."

They proceed to cottages in the village to effect the arrest of others named on the indictment: James Loveless [George's younger brother], Thomas Stan[d]field, John Stan[d]field [his eldest son], James Hammett, and James Brine [not related to the constable].

*1834, 27 February.* The Dorset County Chronicle has printed a typical craft Friendly Society oath of the type that is administered beneath a life-sized painting of a skeleton representing Death: "I do before Almighty God and this loyal lodge most solemnly swear that I will not work for any master that is not in the Union ... nor write to cause to be written either on stone, marble or brass, paper or sand, anything connected with this order, and if ever I reveal any of the rules may what is before me plunge my soul into eternity." By printing this the Dorchester newspaper is making the point that such oaths are commonplace in accepted society.

*1834, 15 March.* The Lent Assize is in session at Dorchester and the six Tolpuddle labourers have been escorted from Dorchester Castle, as its gaol is known, to the cells below the Crown Court at Shire Hall, High West Street. They are brought up to face the judge, Mr Baron Williams [who was recently appointed to the judiciary, being John Williams until 28 February], sitting with a grand jury of magistrates. The labourers are accused of combining together to administer a secret or unlawful oath contrary to the Mutiny Act, 1797. The judge says that the oath was unlawful despite the acceptance by the Crown that the six had not grouped together for any seditious purpose. Edward Legg gives King's evidence that he had been blindfolded before the Lovelesses at an initiation ceremony:

"We were told to keep it secret ... but I don't understand much of what they were saying; we kissed the book directly after repeating the words." The book, apparently, was the Bible. "I know all the prisoners – they are all hard-working men – and I never heard a word against any of them."

Tolpuddle Martyrs' Tree, near Dorchester: ageing symbol of trades unionism, a sycamore, beside which the Dorsetshire Labourers met on Tolpuddle Village Green. Photograph: Colin Graham.

Mr Butt and Mr Derbishire, the defence counsel, argue that the Mutiny Act had been framed to deal with sailors and soldiers, following the mutiny at the Nore, and that the Tolpuddle Friendly Society was not mutinous in its nature or intent. Mr Derbishire describes the Society as a "kind of agricultural savings bank" for needy labourers "to provide against the seasons of scarcity and obviate starvation" rather than an illegal combination.

"Their only crime," he said, "was conspiring to protect each other from the evils of possible starvation."

Mr Gambier, prosecuting, said that such latitude was quite unprecedented.

George Loveless submits a short statement, which is read:

"My lord, if we have violated any law, it was not done intentionally; we have injured no man's reputation, character, person or property. We were uniting together to preserve ourselves, our wives and our children, from utter degradation and starvation."

The jury, however, find a true bill against the prisoners and they are taken down to the cells. Sentence is reserved.

*19th March*. Mr Baron Williams has the six Dorsetshire Labourers brought up from the cells, where they have been for thirty-six hours. The judge says he has been considering the representations of defence counsel but has found them unconvincing:

"The object of all legal punishment is not altogether with the view of operating on the offenders themselves, but with a view to offering an example and a warning."

He pronounces the maximum sentence available: "That you and each of you be transported to such places beyond the seas as His Majesty's Council in their discretion shall see fit for a term of seven years."

Loveless has written out two verses of a radical poem. [It was later printed in his name, as the 'Song of Freedom', though he had remembered the words rather than authored them himself.] The paper falls to the floor and is picked up and handed to the judge. He later has it returned to Loveless:

> "God is our guide, from field, from wave,
> From plough, from anvil, and from loom;
> We come, our country's rights to save,
> And speak any tyrant faction's doom:
> We raise the watch-word Liberty:
> We will, we will, we will be free.

God is our guide! No swords we draw.
We kindle not war's battle fires:
By reason, union, justice, law,
We claim the birth-right of our sires:
We raise the watch-word Liberty:
We will, we will, we will be free."

That night windows in the vicarage at Tolpuddle are broken by stones.

*Footnote:* That was to be about the only protest from Dorset. The rest of the story is elsewhere, with petitions from Parliament, mass demonstrations in London, and the transportations from Gosport and Plymouth. Two years later the government relented and gave free pardons and passages home, but only Hammett would return to finish his life in Tolpuddle. His gravestone is in the churchyard.

*Landscape:* The green, which is a registered village green (VG66, 0.10 hectares), is on a low rise that overlooks the mill stream and the Piddle meadows. In the twentieth century the tree has been lopped and propped.

Major surgery was needed in 1984 and Gill Raikes commented on behalf of the Trust: "One hundred and fifty years later the old tree needs care to keep it alive. The National Trust owns the tree and the land around it, to preserve the site forever. In preparation for the time when the tree will die, a young sapling, taken from the parent, has already been planted so the famous spot will continue to be marked."

Some may think that the tree has not been at all inappropriate as a symbol for the maturing years of trades unionism.

*Trust ownership:* A quarter of an acre given by the lord of the manor. Sir Ernest Debenham, in 1934 – to mark the Martyrs' centenary which was celebrated by a large TUC gathering.

*Location and access:* Tolpuddle village is beside the A35 between Puddletown and Bere Regis, seven miles east of Dorchester. The green is on the junction with the turning, southwards from the centre of the village, between a thatched barn and a row of old cottages.

**Tolpuddle** parish – see **Tolpuddle Martyrs' Tree and Village Green**

**The Training Bank**, Studland – see entry for **Studland Heath National Nature Reserve**

Verney Farm cliffs: the precipitous southern edge of the Isle of Purbeck is a wall of stone, seventy to a hundred feet in height, from Durlston Head at Swanage westwards to St Alban's Head. Photograph: Rodney Legg.

**Tulk's Hill**, Puncknowle – see **West Bexington** entry

**Turf Rick Rock**, Studland – see entry for **Old Harry Rocks**

**Turners Puddle** parish – see entry for **Lawrence of Arabia's Cottage at Clouds Hill**

**Turnworth Down** – see entry for **Ringmoor**

**Turnworth** parish – see entry for **Ringmoor and Turnworth Down**

**Ulwell Gap**, Swanage – see entry for **Godlingston Manor**

Van Dyck – for Flemish painter **Sir Anthony Van Dyck** [1599-1641] see entry for **Kingston Lacy House**

van Raalte – for the effigy of **Charles van Raalte** [1857-1907] see entry for **Brownsea Island**

**VERNEY FARM**
*south of Swanage*                                                    *SZ 009 779*
*Landscape:* Part of the limestone plateau of southern Purbeck, immediately west of the old Swanage quarrylands at the Langton Matravers end of the parish. Sloping coastal grasslands, rising to 400 feet and rich in orchids and other wild flowers, at the top of sheer stone cliffs a hundred feet high.
*Trust ownership:* 150 acres, part of the Corfe Castle Estate bequeathed by Ralph Bankes in 1981.
*Location and access:* A mile and a quarter walk along the cliff path, west from the Dorset County Council's car-park in the Durlston Country Park. You turn south along Swanage seafront for almost as far as you can go. Turn right near the end, up Seymer Road, and then continue uphill into Durlston Road.

The car-park is at the end. You walk westwards along the coastal path, with your back to the Anvil Point lighthouse, and walk the length of the Country Park to a stile in an old stone wall. Next come the three fields of the National Trust's Belle Vue cliffs [*which have their own entry*] and then after one more, narrower field, you cross the boundary into the Verney Farm clifftop.

Together these three public access properties have created a general freedom for you to roam over all but one field of the south-eastern corner of the Isle of Purbeck.

Velazquez – for Spanish painter **Diego Rodriguez de Silva y Velazquez** [1599-1660] see entry for **Kingston Lacy House**

Vespasian – for Roman conqueror of the West Country, later **Emperor Vespasian** [9-79 AD] see entries for **Badbury Rings (and Crab Farm)/ Eggardon Hill/ Hod Hill/** and **Pilsdon Pen**

Victoria – for **Queen Victoria** [1819-1901] see entries for **Studland Village (Cornet Bankes VC)** and **Kingston Lacy House (jubilee monument and tree)**

**Village Greens** – see entries for **Colehill/ Holt/ Pamphill/ Studland/** and **Tolpuddle**

**Vindocladia** – see entry for **Badbury Rings**

Wake – for **Archbishop William Wake** [1657-1737] see entry for **Shapwick Village**

**WARE CLIFFS and DEVONSHIRE HEAD**
*immediately west of Lyme Regis*                    SY 333 917
*Monmouth Beach:* Overlooked from Ware Cliffs, the pebbles of Poker's Pool, immediately west of the mediaeval Cobb harbour, have had this alternative name since the evening of 11 June 1685. James Scott, the Duke of Monmouth, landed here with 82 of his men – to claim the

throne of England from his uncle, James II. They unfurled a green banner with gold embroidered letters: "Fear nothing but God."

The party set off up "the stile path," as Cobb Road was then, and began the ill-fated rebellion that would fail at the Battle of Sedgemoor, in the Somerset Levels, and have its sequel for the vanquished in the Bloody Assize conducted by Lord Chief Justice Jeffreys.

Judge Jeffreys came to Devonshire Head three months after that fateful landing, on 11 September 1685, to see the scaffold that had been prepared for the hanging the following day of his victims, most of whom were to be drawn and quartered so that their remains could be displayed to a wider public.

John Tutchin recorded in 1689 that 12 September 1685 was "a glorious sun shining day" in Lyme Regis. It was seen as a "kind of miracle" that two cart-horses refused to draw the sledge which was to have dragged the condemned men from the town to Devonshire Head. Then it was harnessed to a pair of coach-horses which "broke it in pieces" and the men proceeded on foot.

First to die was Lieutenant-Colonel Abraham Holmes of the Civil War Parliamentary Army, retired, who had his arm shot to pieces in a skirmish at Norton St Philip after which "he laid it on a dresser, and cut it off himself with the cook-maid's knife ... He was hanged on the very spot, where he landed with the Duke."

Christopher Battiscombe was second. A young gentleman, his fiancee had gone on her knees to Judge Jeffreys and begged for him to be spared, to which Jeffreys is said to have replied: "That he could only spare her part of him; but as he knew what she wanted, it should be the part which she liked best, and he would give orders to the sheriff accordingly."

The third to suffer was William Hewling, aged 20, from London, who had landed at Lyme with the Duke as a Lieutenant of Foot. His body, at least, was spared being butchered into sections for distribution around the West Country, as a means of discouraging further rebellion: "The maidens of Lyme, partly by assistance of the populace, and partly through the connivance of the persons in power, buried his remains in Lyme churchyard."

Next it was the turn of Sampson Larke, "learned and dissenting teacher of Lyme," who was refused permission to make a speech, the guard having interrupted him to point out that "the work of the day was so great, they could not afford him time".

Dr Benjamin Temple of Nottingham was, however, allowed his words. He had been engaged by the Duke of Monmouth in Holland as his physician and surgeon.

Sixth in line was Captain Arthur Matthews, a Captain of Foot, who forgave his executioner.

"Life, farewell, thou gaudy dream," was part of the final utterances of Joseph Tyler, a gentleman poet from Bristol: "Painted o'er with grief and joys, which the next short hour destroys."

The eighth prisoner was William Cox, presumably from Lyme as he had the distinction of being the first man to enlist in the rebel army, after the Duke landed in the town.

Ninth to hang was Charmouth fisherman Samuel Robins who went on board the Duke's ship to sell fish and was then "compelled to pilot him into Lyme". It seems he would have been pardoned except that a copy of a seditious book, *The Solemn League and Covenant*, had been found at his house.

Nothing is known about the tenth victim, Josias Ascue.

Captain John Madders, Constable of Crewkerne, was another who was said to have almost escaped with his life. Someone then praised him at his trial as a "good protestant". "Oho!" says Jeffreys. "He is a presbyterian. I can smell them forty miles. He shall be hanged."

Finally came the turn of Captain John Kidd who had spent the whole day witnessing the "dreadful sight" of the killing and dismembering of the eleven who had gone before.

*Cement works:* This stood to the south of the Trust's fields, with its chimneys set into the cliff beside Monmouth Beach, and made hydraulic cement – a specialist product used in Victorian and Edwardian harbour-works that hardened under water. Stucco was also made here for decorative wall-facings.

Eleanore Coade, who manufactured Regency terracotta mouldings, built Belmont House [now John Fowles's home] at the top end of Cobb Road, Lyme Regis. She died in about 1820 and has been linked with the establishment of this cement works though all the larger items that were given the firm's imprint proclaim "COADE LAMBETH" and the business was based there, in London, at Pedlar's Acre.

As for the Lyme Cement Works, it was demolished early in the twentieth century. The surviving industrial archaeology consists of sluices and a dam, for the reservoir for the water used in the process of heating the lias clays, and these are still visible on the Trust's lands.

*Landscape:* Flower-rich rough pasture, its diversity enhanced by past landslips, with a fine view of Lyme Bay and the sweep of the Chesil Beach to Portland.

The Knap, the western clifftop field, has large hybridised dactylorchid colonies and sporadic bee orchids as well as the nearest cowslips to Lyme. There is also ragged robin and evening primrose. Stonechats breed here and butterflies occur in profusion. Bluebells smother the centre of the Trust's lands and badger tracks are evident across them, from sets in the nearby scrub.

*Trust ownership:* 29.42 acres of which 0.15 acres are in Devon, formerly part of Ramscombe Farm, bought in 1987 through an appeal launched by novelist John Fowles and the Lyme Regis Society, supported by the Miss M. Howard Bequest and the Nature Conservancy Council.

*Location and access:* Immediately south-west of Lyme Regis, sandwiched between the town and the Dorset–Devon county boundary at Ware.

Three public footpaths cross the Trust's land. The easiest approach is to park in the large Holmbush car-park beside the A3052 at the top end of Cobb Road. Lyme Regis footpath number 13, known as Pine Walk, leads out of the car-park on the south-west side. Its trees are Corsican pines, twenty-two of them. The Trust's land begins after the houses.


Waugh – for runaway banker **Colonel William Petrie Waugh** [nineteenth century] see entry for **Brownsea Island**


Wellesley – for architect **Gerald Wellesley** [later seventeenth Duke of Wellington, 1885-1972] see entry for **Portland House**


Wellington – for "the Iron Duke" **Arthur Wellesley, first Duke of Wellington** [1769-1852] see entry for **Kingston Lacy House**


Wells – for author and futurist **Herbert George Wells** [1866-1946] see

West Bexington, near Abbotsbury: the limekiln of Limekiln Hill, restored by the National Trust and one of the best preserved Dorset examples of these once commonplace structures that produced lime for building and agricultural purposes. Photograph: Colin Graham.

entry for **Old Harry Rocks**

## WEST BEXINGTON, LIMEKILN HILL, TULK'S HILL, LABOUR-IN-VAIN FARM, and THE CHESIL BEACH
*west of Abbotsbury*                                            *SY 547 867*

*Bronze Age burial mounds* (westwards from *SY 544 868*): Group of several well preserved round barrows strung along the skyline at Tulk's Hill, dating from about 2,000 BC in the Bronze Age.

*Limekiln (SY 540 870):* Limekiln Hill has the undulations of limestone quarries, into the iron-stained beds that give Abbotsbury its rich colours, and its name comes from the kiln which survives at the edge of the escarpment. Dating from the early nineteenth century it produced building mortar and limewash. It would have been filled from the top with alternating layers of stone and wood, the slow combustion converting the rock into quicklime.

*Pillboxes:* In the fields and beside the beach are concrete emplacements that were the anti-invasion defences of 1940.

*The name:* Labour-in-Vain is one of those Dorset names that evokes an image of perpetual exhaustion for zero rewards. It is a reminder that before the days of tractors and subsidies farming was not much fun on the thin soils beside an exposed shoreline. Nearby, in contrast, is a farm known as Peace and Plenty.

*Landscape:* The ridge has fine views over Lyme Bay and down to the Chesil Beach, a stretch of which is in the Trust's ownership to the west of the former Abbotsbury Coastguard Station. Grain is grown between the beach and the hills but the escarpment is reserved for rough grazing and roe deer, with extensive scrubland on Tulk's Hill. Some young oaks were planted in memory of Dennis Cosgrove [1924-80], an Australian scientist who researched inositol phosphates but maintained a lifelong enthusiasm for the Dorset countryside.

*Trust ownership:* 262 acres. Limekiln Hill was given by Sir Ronald Milne Watson in 1964, and an additional twenty acres bought in 1965-70 with moneys from Mrs Ella Corbett. The 225 acres of Labour-in-Vain Farm came to the Trust from the Treasury in 1979, through the National Land Fund.

*Location and access:* The ridge is beside the B3157 Bridport to Weymouth coast road, between Swyre and Abbotsbury, and there is

Whitecliff Farm and Swanage Bay: a view in the 1890s, before suburbia advanced, but National Trust fields now prevent it from sprawling to the foot of Ballard Down. Photograph: John Pouncy.

parking at Limekiln Hill.

At Labour-in-Vain, to the west of old Abbotsbury Coastguard Station, the Trust owns a section of the famous Chesil Beach. This is beside the Burton Road, a public highway which runs immediately inland of the Chesil Beach from Abbotsbury Sub Tropical Gardens (first turning seaward to the west of the village) to West Bexington. It is unwise to drive along it because much of its length is rutted, covered with shingle, or otherwise hostile for vehicles. A more sensible approach is to turn south off the B3157 at Swyre to the car-park in West Bexington. Walk half a mile eastwards along the coast path. Public paths cross the fields to Labour-in-Vain and the ridge at Limekiln Hill and Tulk's Hill. Keep to the public footpaths on this tenanted farmland.

**West Cliff**, Chideock – see entry for **Seatown**

**West Hawes**, Corfe Castle – see entry for **Corfe Common**

**West Hill**, Corfe Castle – see entry for **Corfe Common**

**Westwood Farm**, Corfe Castle – see entry for **Ailwood Down**

**Weymouth** borough – see entry for **Portland House**

**Whit[e]church Canonicorum** parish – see entries for **Coney's Castle/ Hardown Hill/ Saint Wite's Well and Ship Farm/** and **Newlands Batch** (listed under **Stonebarrow Hill**)

## WHITECLIFF FARM, BALLARD DOWN, and PUNFIELD COVE
*north of Swanage*                                              *SZ 030 810*

*Punfield Cove (SZ 040 810)*: The dip in the undercliff at the Swanage end of the chalk on Ballard Cliff [not named by the Ordnance Survey, but known locally as Punfield] is of considerable geological interest. It is highly fossiliferous and contains the Punfield marine band which has Spanish affinities. This lies in the cretaceous layers, of the final Mesozoic period, when the lower greensand and colourful Wealden sands were accumulating in the warm waters.

*Bronze Age burial mounds (SZ 040 813)*: There are eight skyline round barrows on Ballard Down, which were raised to cover aristocratic burials about 1,800 BC. Three were opened by John Austen in 1851 and he returned to do another trio in 1857. The hollows at the centre of the mounds are his mark.

Underneath he found crouched skeletons, with one such primary burial under each mound. and pieces of antler-pick which had been used to quarry the chalk. Later Bronze Age burials had been inserted in some of the mounds, in the form of cremations, and from these Austen found urn fragments. There was also the burial of a child in a pit that had been cut into the chalk.

Several of the mounds were damaged by Second World War defences, apparently for a radar apparatus, and they have been subsequently virtually levelled by ploughing.

*Strip lynchets* (*SZ 028 807*): Three mediaeval raised strip fields survive in a poor condition north-west of Whitecliff Farm, and this open field formerly extended to the foot of Ballard Down. There was a Saxon settlement at Whitecliff, listed by the Normans in their Domesday Survey of 1086.

*Boundary stones* (westwards from *SZ 040 813*): Eight eighteenth century boundary stones, along the fenceline of Ballard Down, mark the limits of "SM" [Swanage Manor] and the parish of Studland. The second stone from the east, 250 yards west from the main cluster of barrows, is dated 1776.

*Landscape:* The 500 feet high chalk spine of Ballard Down stretches for well over a mile and has fine views in all directions.

Southwards the view is over the Swanage valley and northwards it is across the heath and harbour to Poole and Bournemouth. Seawards the panorama brings in Studland Bay, the cliffs to the entrance of The Solent, and then the whole western side of the Isle of Wight from The Needles to St Catherine's Point.

The south-facing chalk escarpments have a disappointing flora as the extremes of heat and dryness are too much for most herbs.

*Trust ownership:* 222 acres, bought with Enterprise Neptune appeal funds in 1976, but excluding the actual farmhouse.

*Location and access:* There are public footpaths to Whitecliff Farm and Punfield [the latter being beside the coastal footpath] from Hill Road and Ballard Road at the northern edge of Swanage.

Alternatively you can park in the large layby beside the mosaic of glazed tiles that depict "Swanage" on the Swanage–Studland road at the south side of the Ulwell Gap. From here you follow the public path notices, around the reservoir, to the top of Ballard Down. There is a path down to Whitecliff Farm, on the south side in about half a mile, and another to Punfield Cove in a further half mile.

**White Hill Plantation**, Chedington – see entry for **Winyard's Gap**

**White Mill**, Shapwick – see entry for **Shapwick Village**

**White Mill Bridge**, Shapwick – see entry for **Shapwick Village**

**White Nothe**, Owermoigne – see entry for **South Down Farm**

**The Wilderness**, Langton Matravers – see entry for **Wilkswood Farm**

## WILKSWOOD FARM, TALBOT'S WOOD, LANGTON WEST WOOD, THE WILDERNESS, GODLINGSTON WOOD, WOODHOUSE HILL, and other PURBECK AMENITY WOODLAND

*principally to the north of Langton Matravers, with other woodlands at Godlingston and Studland*

*SY 996 796*

*Woodhouse Hill Roman Buildings, Studland* (*SZ 031 822*): A substantial group of buildings cover a considerable area, upwards of 1,600 square yards – the size of a modern farm – in the eastern part of the wood on Woodhouse Hill, Studland. Two clusters of heathstone and flint foundations were uncovered by Norman Field in 1952-58.

The walls were up to three feet thick and probably supported cob walls. The site had a long life and was most likely still occupied in the early fourth century. One northern room, at least, was built at that time as it had a coin of the British usurper Allectus [293-96] beneath the floor. The next building had five coins of the second half of the third century [259-96].

South of this building was the remains of a much earlier circular hut which had been flanked with sheds on all sides. A Samian platter, a high-quality import, lay on a low clay shelf on the west side, and was dated to 65-80 AD. There also was a coin of Vespasian [AD 73] and crucibles for bronze-working. Lesser remains of a similar hut and workshops were found to the south of the entrance to the later building to the east.

The main southern group of buildings, 80 feet closer to the road, also had a long and complicated history. Underlying the east–west rectangles of third century buildings was a room of the late first century AD, aligned north-west to south-east.

*Roman Marble Industry* (*SY 996 795*): Surface workings and shallow quarries north of Langton Matravers at Wilkswood are, some of them, among the most ancient workings in Dorset. Here the Romans worked marble, favouring the greyish-white variety, and used it to form a smart speckled background to the vermillion lettering in cinnabar. This style was widely used in Roman monumental inscriptions and such tables of marble have been unearthed from Fordington in Dorset and as far afield as Chester, Chichester, Cirencester, London, Colchester and St Albans.

One slab of Purbeck stone, broken in half, is in the Corinium Museum at Cirencester. It was originally seven feet high and had its lettering picked out in red. When the central altar of the great temple of Claudius at Colchester was rebuilt, after the uprising of Boudica in AD 60-61, it appears to have been covered with Purbeck marble, as its excavators found slabs of marble across the cellar floor. Roman tombstones also tended to be very large.

Another use of Purbeck marble and stone was for mortars, the stone withstanding hard grinding and pounding. This was of crucial importance to the economy of the Roman province of Britannia. The major technological innovation in Roman Britain was the rotary quern – large numbers of which were cut from Purbeck stone – which enabled the efficient grinding of corn, expanding the country's food supply and consequently its population. Before the corn had been crushed between two stones. The difference in production levels were sufficient to turn Britain into a grain exporting state, to the continental legions on the Rhine.

Marble also appears decoratively, used in panels and for moulded friezes in important buildings – even, at Silchester, for large basins in the public baths. Roman marble workings in Purbeck appear to have flourished during two periods: from AD 43 to 150, and again between AD 350 and 400. Of all the many quarries opened for building stone in Roman Britain, the Purbeck sites were most specialised and existed solely for luxury purposes, which is why the trade thrived during times of extensive building and, later, had a second life during the country's economic revival.

*Mediaeval Wilkswood Quarries (SY 994 795):* The Trust's woodlands in the valley north of Langton Matravers, on the slopes to the south of the stream, also conceal thirteenth century marble workings which provided building stone for cathedrals and effigies for the distinguished dead of much of Britain. Some of the stone was exported to Ireland and the continent.

It is not a true marble but a vein of highly fossiliferous freshwater limestone that cuts smooth and takes a polish. The sites of the workings and their sledge tracks are beneath an eerie tangle of undergrowth in the valley, from Wilkswood Farm through Langton West Wood and westward towards Primrose Hill.

*Landscape:* The main belt of ancient deciduous woodland in the Isle of Purbeck is on the Trust's lands around Wilkswood Farm. It includes Langton West Wood to the west, and The Wilderness to the north beside the railway line.

Godlingston Wood is another patch of older woodland, on the spring-line to the north of the ancient manor house [*see entry for Godlingston Manor*].

Woodhouse Hill at Studland is also elderly remnant tree-cover, on a spur of sandstone at the 200 feet contour between the main heath and the open, rolling chalklands on the north slopes of Ballard Down. The Trust also owns the other small woods around Studland but these are mainly recent plantations.

*Trust ownership:* 254 acres of amenity woodland were part of the Corfe Castle Estate left to the Trust by Ralph Bankes in 1982.

*Location and access:* The principal batch of ancient woodlands, to the north of Langton Matravers, are reached from the lane on the north side of the B3069 a hundred yards west from the village schools. This becomes a path in a third of a mile, after the last buildings, and tracks branch off to the left towards Primrose Hill and to the right to Talbot's Wood. If you continue straight ahead for another third of a mile, you come to the valley bottom and cross the stream. Then, in a hundred yards, you cross another public highway. This is a bridleway which to the left skirts Langton West Wood and leads to Quarr [the Dorset dialect word for the business].

To the right the bridleway runs along the northern side of the valley above Wilkswood Farm. The alternative is to continue straight ahead, for a quarter of a mile, to the small but aptly named woodland, The Wilderness, overlooking the cutting of the Swanage Railway which was reconstructed in the late 1980s.

Godlingston Wood (*SZ 015 805*) is beside a public path that runs northwards from the track that branches off the lane, on the north side, between the cemetery and Godlingston Manor. There is a small lake at the south end of the woods. These extend around a semi-circular coombe at the foot of the Purbeck Hills.

Woodhouse Hill (*SZ 030 823*) lies on the north side of the main road into Studland, 250 yards from the edge of the village. The villa or workshops, some slight walls of which remain, is seventy yards up the slope near the eastern boundary of the wood.

## WINYARD'S GAP, CRATE'S COPPICE, PENNEY'S HILL COPPICE, WHITE HILL PLANTATION, and NORTH HILL PLANTATION
*above Chedington*                                                    ST 491 061

*Memorial* (*ST 491 060*): To the war dead of the 43rd (Wessex) Division of the Territorial Army in the campaign from Normandy to the Baltic, 1944-45. It is a replica of the memorial on Point 112 behind the D-Day beach-head at Caen and is one of a number unveiled on West Country hilltops in 1952.

Point 112 was the hill south-west of Caen, between Esquay and Eterville, which the 43rd Division, including the 4th Battalion of the Dorsetshire Regiment, attacked at 05.00 hours on 10 July 1944. They took the hill but were driven out of the nearby village of Maltot by a strong German counter-attack and on 11 July had to hold Point 112 against an onslaught from the 10th SS Panzer Division.

Above the inscription at Chedington is a square plaque featuring the 43rd Division's dragonesque Wessex wyvern emblem.

*Name:* 'Wynheard' – a Saxon personal name. 'Gap' – the pass through the hills which has been a main road for centuries. Charles I passed through it in 1644 and, it was observed, "he rode the great horse very well".

*Literary associations:* 'The Three Horseshoes', as the Winyard's Gap Inn was known, feature in *The Clear State of the Case of Elizabeth Canning*, a rare 1752 pamphlet by Henry Fielding concerning a notorious gipsy-alibi trial. Canning may have been the victim or

222

**Winyard's Gap, Chedington: surmounted by a memorial to the 43rd (Wessex) Division and the 1944-45 campaign from Normandy to the Baltic. It features their wyvern emblem above the inscription. Photograph: Colin Graham.**

villain, kidnapped or prostitute. At any event she was convicted and transported. Mary Squires was either abductress or scapegoat – innocent gypsy or brothel matron. The jury thought the worse and she was sentenced to hang but this was pardoned.

*Landscape:* Dense, south-facing, woodland on the escarpment above Winyard's Gap where the road climbs a deep cutting into a lip of the Dorset Downs. This is a fine viewpoint, from 800 feet, over two distinct regions.

To the west the valley of the River Axe (which begins as a trickle less than a mile from here) winding between the hills of Dorset and Somerset before slipping into Devon. Eastward is the gathering flatness that becomes the Blackmore Vale, interspersed with ripples of undistinguished hilliness that fail to compete with the solid line of the chalk escarpment.

*Trust ownership:* 16 acres, given in 1949 as a memorial to the 43rd Division.

*Location and access:* The A356 road from Maiden Newton to Crewkerne drops from above the 800 feet contour to only 200 feet in a two mile stretch at Chedington.

Turn towards Chedington at the Winyard's Gap Inn. After the next small block of trees, beyond the public house, there is another small car-park from which a footpath leads up the hill to the memorial.

**Woodhouse Hill**, Studland – see entry for **Wilkswood Farm**

**Worth Matravers** parish – see entry for **Seacombe Bottom and Eastington Farm**


## SELF-INDEXED — ENTRIES ARE ALPHABETICAL !
Listings are under MAJOR PROPERTY HEADINGS
with cross-referencing for 'minor' properties,
people associated with them, and short-lists
of Trust-owned land in each parish and borough.